MARVEL

THE WAY OF THE WARRIOR

MARVEL'S MIGHTIEST MARTIAL ARTISTS

MARVEL
THE WAY OF THE WARRIOR
MARVEL'S MIGHTIEST MARTIAL ARTISTS
WRITTEN BY
ALAN COWSILL

CONTENTS

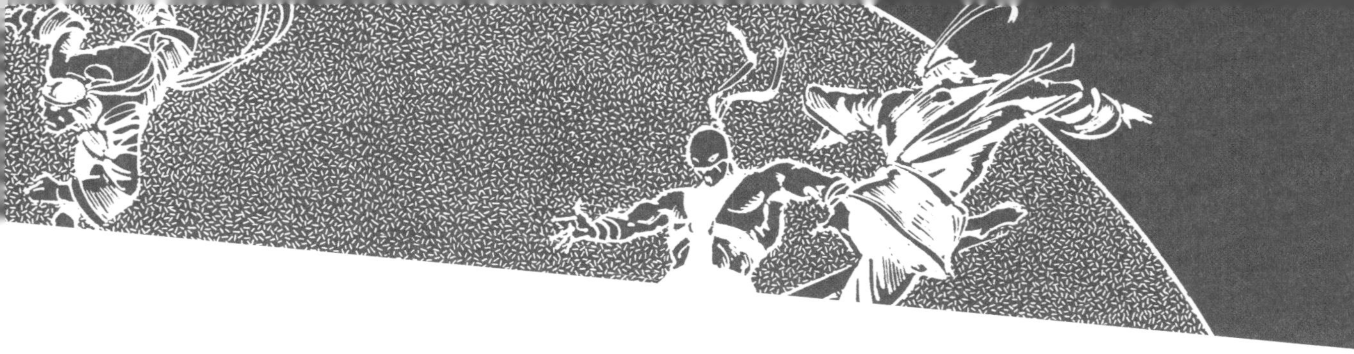

INTRODUCTION

I fell in love with martial arts at an early age. Like most kids growing up in the UK in the early 1970s, for me, Bruce Lee was the king—both a hero and role model, with the entire world seemingly "kung-fu fighting." I might have been too young to watch *Enter the Dragon,* but every kid in my school knew who Bruce Lee was. Likewise the Lee-inspired TV show *Kung Fu* popularized the art. Marvel, as always, was at the forefront of this pop-culture phenomena—with Shang-Chi and Iron Fist leading the way. I started practicing martial arts at college, beginning with a few years of praying mantis and then, after a long gap, wing chun. Even when I wasn't training I remained in love with martial arts and martial arts characters, and Marvel has created some of the comic book medium's greatest martial arts heroes and villains. From Shang-Chi and Iron Fist through to the Daughters of the Dragon and Daredevil, martial arts has proven to be central to some of Marvel's greatest-ever stories.

There are a lot of Marvel characters and a surprising number are martial artists. For this book we wanted to select the best of the best. After a long and tough selection process, we settled on those associated with martial arts stemming from the East, rather than Western fighting arts such as boxing and wrestling. These are the heroes and villains who follow a moral code (albeit sometimes a twisted one) and fight a certain way. While many heroes and villains have super-powers and exceptional abilities, only a select few have chosen the Way of the Warrior...

ALAN COWSILL

MARTIAL ARTS MASTERS

SHANG-CHI

CHAMPION OF THE DEADLY HAND

While Shang-Chi is regarded as the world's greatest martial arts hero, it wasn't supposed to be that way. Centuries ago, his father and uncle, the ancient sorcerers Zheng Zu and Zheng Yi, created a warrior sect known as the Five Weapons Society to protect China. Their aims were noble, but after Zheng Yi died, his brother took a darker path. He sought to dominate the world and return China to its old ways, using the Five Weapons Society to accomplish his goals. Shang-Chi was raised in Zheng Zu's hidden compound in Hunan Province with the intention that he would one day lead one of the houses of the Five Weapons Society—the House of the Deadly Hand.

Zheng Zu understood that to be a true master of the martial arts, one also needed to master one's own mind; he not only brought the world's greatest martial artists to train his son, but also the greatest scholars. However, the philosophy and morality Shang-Chi learned conflicted with his father's aims. Eventually Shang-Chi was forced to break away and forge his own path, often opposing his father's evil machinations.

Over time, Shang-Chi's reputation grew. Whether he was caught up in MI-6's games of death and deceit or fighting as an Avenger against beings far more powerful, Shang-Chi was always true to his art, even though at times it was at great personal cost. He became a teacher and hero, constantly striving to improve his skills—the living embodiment of the very essence of martial arts. While heroes such as Iron Fist and Daredevil are fighters of great renown, in a troubled and dangerous world there is only one true master of the martial arts, and his name is Shang-Chi.

AVENGERS #11 (JUL. 2013) Trained by his father to be the world's greatest martial artist and a leader of the Five Weapons Society, Shang-Chi rebelled and chose to use his deadly skills as a force for good.

The Spirit Rises

The son of Zheng Zu, one of the world's most notorious sorcerers, Shang-Chi was raised in seclusion at his father's hidden compound in Hunan Province, China.

As a child, Shang-Chi believed his father to be a heroic figure with plans to save mankind. Though this was a lie, Zheng Zu had in fact once been a force for good. He worked tirelessly with his younger brother, Zheng Yi, to protect China from internal and external threats. To that end, the two sorcerers had created the Five Weapons Society. The Society was made up of five houses, each specializing in a different weapon. They were the House of the Deadly Staff; the House of the Deadly Sabre; the House of the Deadly Dagger; the House of the Deadly Hammer; and the House of the Deadly Hand.

During the Opium Wars, Zheng Yi was severely injured in battle. Zheng Zu wanted to use the Eyes of the Dragon, an ancient mystical artifact, to restore his younger brother's life and energy—at the cost of his own. Yi refused and instead gave his own life essence to the artifact, empowering Zheng Zu who went on to avenge Yi's death. But without his younger brother to provide balance, Zheng Zu's methods started to darken. He became sadistic and violent, even executing his own warriors when they failed him. He allowed people to believe he had killed his brother to increase his own dark reputation and started to use sorcery and science to create monstrous creatures to advance his plans. He moved the five houses to secret locations across the world, leaving only one—the Deadly Hand—in China.

SHANG-CHI #1 (NOV. 2020) Centuries ago, the Five Weapons Society, led by Zheng Zu and Zheng Yi, served as protectors for the Chinese people.

Left: SHANG-CHI #2 (DEC. 2020) Shang-Chi and Shi-Hua uncovered gruesome evidence of their father's plans.

Below right: SHANG-CHI #2 (DEC. 2020) Shang-Chi believed his sister had been killed for her insolence. Despite this, he was true to his word and remained in his father's compound.

Shang-Chi was raised in the Hunan retreat with his sister, Shi-Hua. Cut off from the world, Zheng Zu made his children and students live according to Qing Dynasty ways. One night, when Shang-Chi was young, he and his sister were searching for crystal cakes when they stumbled across one of their father's laboratories where he was trying to create undead servants. A furious Zheng Zu was about to kill Shi-Hua when Shang-Chi promised to obey him completely if only he would show his sister mercy. Shang-Chi didn't see his sister again for 15 years, and believed she had been granted a quick, merciful death by Zheng Zu.

Shang-Chi had the greatest masters in the world to teach him both martial arts and philosophy—even Shang-Chi's name meant the "advancing and rising of the spirit." He remained true to his word and obeyed his father's wishes unconditionally, until he came to realize just how immoral they were. Appalled by his father's plans for world domination, Shang-Chi was forced to strike out on his own and fight his father's evil. Shang-Chi became his father's greatest enemy—and the world's greatest martial artist.

YOUR SISTER IS *GONE*, SHANG-CHI.
BUT TAKE COMFORT IN KNOWING THAT I HONORED YOUR REQUEST. I SHOWED *MERCY*.

Games of Deceit and Death

After learning the truth about his father's criminal empire, Shang-Chi found himself alone in New York.

His father longed to return China to its older ways and had raised his son in a compound with no access to modern technology. Although it had made him a master of the martial arts, Shang-Chi's upbringing had left him totally unprepared for the modern world. In New York, however, Shang-Chi soon found allies and friends—mostly those opposed to his father's ways. He teamed up with super-powered beings such as Spider-Man and Man-Thing, while his martial arts skills led to friendships with Iron Fist, the Sons of the Tiger, and the Daughters of the Dragon.

Before Shang-Chi had time to settle into his new surroundings, he was attacked by Midnight, a deadly assassin who also happened to be one of Shang-Chi's few childhood friends. Midnight's real name was M'Nai, and he had been raised alongside Shang-Chi like a brother. M'Nai had taken a darker path in life and had been sent to kill Shang-Chi. Their first confrontation raged through New York and only ended when Midnight fell to his death from a crane. He was later resurrected by Kree technology and returned as Midnight Sun to further plague Shang-Chi.

Shang-Chi teamed up with Spider-Man again a few years later, the pair helping Nick Fury and Black Widow prevent an attempt by Viper and the Silver Samurai to kill the President. His martial arts skills also brought him to the attention of the British Intelligence service, MI-6. Believing Shang-Chi to still be an assassin, MI-6 sent an ex-army agent by the name of Black Jack Tarr to kill him. Tarr failed, and realizing their mistake, MI-6 tried to recruit Shang-Chi instead.

Opposite: MASTER OF KUNG FU OMNIBUS #3 (MAR. 2017) After Shang-Chi broke away from his father's control, he soon found himself with deadly allies in MI-6.

Below: MASTER OF KUNG FU #19 (AUG. 1974) Shang-Chi first met the monstrous Man-Thing while trying to escape from assassins in the Florida Everglades.

MASTER OF KUNG FU #48 (JAN. 1978)
Black Jack Tarr was working for MI-6 when he first met Shang-Chi. He later became the agency's director.

Shang-Chi refused MI-6's offer, but agreed to help them take down drug dealer Carlton Velcro. While Black Jack Tarr was often dismissive of Shang-Chi, in time, bonds of respect grew between the pair. Shang-Chi respected the older man's loyalty and exceptional—if sometimes brutal—fighting technique.

While working alongside MI-6, Shang-Chi also made the acquaintance of British spy Clive Reston. Reston's great uncle had been an exceptionally talented detective with an uncanny knack for deductive reasoning, while his father had worked in Her Majesty's Secret Service with a license to kill. Reston had inherited his great uncle's detective skills and his father's deadly talent. While Shang-Chi appreciated Reston's abilities, he often disliked his dark humor.

The most important ally in Shang-Chi's life also became his lover. Leiko Wu was one of MI-6's top operatives and one of the few people whose fighting skills rivaled those of Shang-Chi. When they first met, Leiko had only recently left Clive Reston for another agent, Simon Bretnor. When it appeared that a deadly assassin called Mordillo had kidnapped Bretnor, Leiko went to rescue him—only to learn that Bretnor was actually Mordillo. The assassin was obsessed with her and took Leiko back to his island base where he planned to unleash "Project Ultraviolet" on the world, a top secret British experiment to use solar warfare against its enemies. Shang-Chi joined his new allies in a rescue attempt. Mordillo's island base was a twisted reflection of the assassin's deranged mind, filled with strange and almost childlike robots and traps. The assassin was not only a crazed inventor but also an exceptional martial artist.

Shang-Chi and Reston fought their way across Mordillo's island only to be captured by the madman and strapped to chairs in a theater, where

"You have both lived within games of deceit for so long that you no longer know what the truth is."

SHANG-CHI

they were forced to watch Leiko face certain death, trapped in a giant hourglass. Luckily Black Jack Tarr came to their aid, disguised as one of Mordillo's robotic assassins. His intervention allowed Shang-Chi to escape his bonds and free Leiko from the death trap.

There had been an instant attraction between Leiko and Shang-Chi and this grew stronger when he rescued her. Shang-Chi and his allies went on to help destroy Mordillo's solar weapon, the villain himself dying in the blast. In the aftermath, Shang-Chi gave in to his attraction to Leiko. The pair soon became lovers—much to Reston's resentment—and Shang-Chi found himself increasingly pulled into Leiko's world of deceit and death while also facing increasingly strange and dangerous enemies.

MASTER OF KUNG FU #47 (DEC. 1976)
Leiko Wu, a British-Chinese MI-6 agent, was also an exceptional martial artist, and would often train with Shang-Chi.

MASTER OF KUNG FU #38 (MAR. 1976) Shen Kuei gained the name of "the Cat" due to his cunning, skill, and stealth.

Left: **MASTER OF KUNG FU #105 (OCT. 1981)** Following the original's death, two other Razor-Fists worked for Velcro's Assassination Bureau.

Deadly Foes of Kung Fu

The world of international espionage brought Shang-Chi into conflict with some of the deadliest villains on Earth. He faced killers such as Razor-Fist, Shockwave, Zaran the Weapons Master, and the Cat—the one martial artist he could not defeat.

Early on in Shang-Chi's relationship with Black Jack Tarr and his allies, Shang-Chi helped them in an attempt to bring drug lord Carlton Velcro to justice. When the heroes launched a raid on Velcro's island base, Shang-Chi found himself pitted against Velcro's personal bodyguard, William Young, better known as Razor-Fist. Already a formidable martial artist, Young's hands had been replaced with lethal blades. He was fighting Shang-Chi when Velcro ordered his men to open fire, their bullets killing Young. In the aftermath, Velcro turned two brothers, Douglas and William Scott, into Razor-Fists. Velcro accidentally killed William during

MASTER OF KUNG FU #39 (APR. 1976) During his first showdown with the Cat, Shang-Chi used his signature nunchaku against Shen Kuei's lethal guandao.

a showdown with Shang-Chi, but Douglas survived. Douglas made the Razor-Fist identity his own and had several further run-ins with Shang-Chi.

Some villains, such as Shockwave, used advanced technology to enhance their martial arts abilities. Shockwave was Lancaster Sneed, the nephew of one of MI-6's leading operatives. He created an exoskeleton for himself that used electricity to shock and kill his opponents. He relied on his technology too much, though, and was easily defeated by Shang-Chi.

Not all of those Shang-Chi faced could be described as villains. His greatest foe was also one that walked a morally gray area. Shen Kuei was better known as the Cat, and as a martial arts master, his skills rivaled those of Shang-Chi. Their first meeting occurred when Shang-Chi was sent to Hong Kong to rescue an agent named Juliette and retrieve stolen MI-6 papers from Shen Kuei. When Shang-Chi approached Juliette in the Jade Peacock bar, he learned that her life wasn't in danger from Shen, and that she had fallen in love with him. The Cat mistakenly believed Juliette had betrayed him to MI-6 and sought out Shang-Chi, arriving at the bar just as some street punks were about to attack the martial arts master. Honor dictated that the Cat help his would-be enemy, the two martial artists acknowledging each other's skill as they cleared the bar. The following day, after Shang-Chi learned that the documents he had been sent for didn't actually belong to the British, the Cat returned—still convinced that Juliette had betrayed him and that Shang-Chi sought his death. For his part, Shang-Chi realized that MI-6 had played him and used him as one of their operatives—a scenario he had wanted to avoid. The two masters started their confrontation, neither giving an inch. The fight only ended when Juliette intervened and forced a conclusion by stabbing herself. The act brought Shen to his senses and he stood down to help Juliette, realizing just how much he loved her. In their future encounters, Shang-Chi and Shen would often find themselves on opposing sides but always respected each other's skill and honor.

MASTER OF KUNG FU #69 (OCT. 1978) Skull Crusher was an expert martial artist whose favorite weapons were two meteor hammers—chains with heavy balls at their ends.

MASTER OF KUNG FU #77 (JUN. 1979) Maximilian Zaran was a master of countless weapons. He often fought with a number of small sai blades attached to his costume.

Shang-Chi tried to sever his connections to MI-6, but fate—in the form of new enemy Shaka Kharn—again compelled him to join forces with Black Jack Tarr, Clive Reston, and Leiko. As they fought to stop a maniac from using missiles to blow the Moon from Earth's orbit, Shang-Chi found himself facing Kharn, a deadly warrior who was one of Shang-Chi's ancestors, raised from the dead. As they fought, Shang-Chi was shocked when his enemy's helm fell off revealing a skeletal form, his rebirth incomplete. Shaka Kharn came close to killing Shang-Chi, but ultimately failed, Shang-Chi beheading his half-human form.

When Shang-Chi again became tangled up with the Cat, he found himself facing a mercenary called Skull Crusher, an exceptional martial artist who used flails to make his attacks even deadlier. The mercenary, whose real name was Chao Sima, would return again and again to menace Shang-Chi, but eventually redeemed himself after falling in love with Leiko Wu. He tried to use the ill-gotten gains from a criminal clan he had taken over to establish an orphanage, but was killed by Midnight Sun, only to return from the dead to gain vengeance on his killer.

Another of Shang-Chi's deadly foes was Zaran the Weapons Master, who had started out as an MI-6 agent before going rogue. A master of all weaponry and a talented martial artist, he proved to be one of Shang-Chi's most lethal enemies. Zaran went on to become a mercenary, teaming up with French mercenary Batroc and South American revolutionary Machete as part of Batroc's Brigade, and launched an ultimately unsuccessful bid to steal Captain America's shield. He also took on the occasional student and one of these, Zhou Man She, adopted the name of Zaran himself, believing himself to be his teacher's superior, and tried to create a criminal empire only to be defeated by Shang-Chi.

In time, Shang-Chi and his allies quit MI-6 and formed Freelance Restorations, a covert group that aimed to help those in need. Shang-Chi and Leiko infiltrated the Cult of the Dawning Light while part of Freelance Restorations, helping to end the cult, which had been created by former KGB agents seeking to damage western civilization. He was forced to fight alongside MI-6 on several more occasions, but Shang-Chi always parted ways with his allies as soon as the threat passed, tired of their games of death and deceit. He became a fisherman, before settling in a remote temple to pass on his skills and wisdom to others, but it wasn't long before the past again sought him out.

MASTER OF KUNG FU #49 (FEB. 1977)
Shaka Kharn needed to take on special nutrients to remain alive. Without them, he returned to a more skeletal form.

Moving Shadow

After his ex-lover disappeared, Shang-Chi was pulled back into action when he found himself facing an assassin trained from birth with only one aim: to kill him.

Shang-Chi was at peace. After years of constant fighting, the martial arts master had turned his back on the world of espionage, choosing to live a quiet life of beauty and serenity on an island, and content to pass on his knowledge and skills to others. That all changed when Shang-Chi's former lover, Leiko Wu, was captured on a mission for MI-6. Her husband and fellow agent Clive Reston turned to Shang-Chi for help rescuing her. Leiko had gone missing while investigating the mysterious Saint Germain, an immortal mastermind—also known as the Ghost—who had inherited a vast criminal empire. It was enough to draw the martial arts master back into the fray. He soon found himself the target of an assassin named Moving Shadow, although the attempt failed.

SHANG-CHI: MASTER OF KUNG FU #1 (NOV. 2002) While finally at peace on his island retreat, Shang-Chi tried to teach his hard-earned life lessons to others.

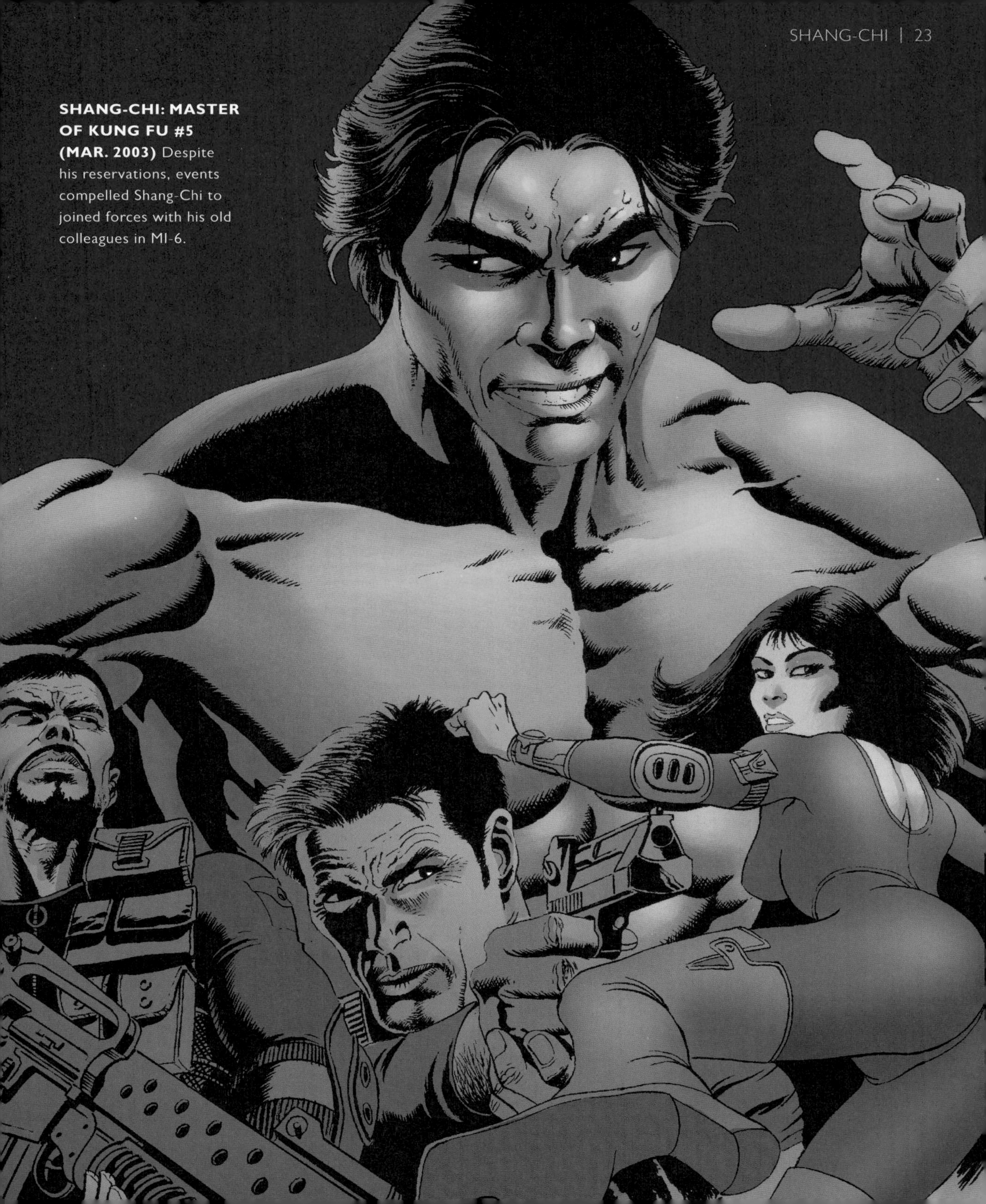

SHANG-CHI: MASTER OF KUNG FU #5 (MAR. 2003) Despite his reservations, events compelled Shang-Chi to joined forces with his old colleagues in MI-6.

SHANG-CHI: MASTER OF KUNG FU #6 (APR. 2003) In their final confrontation, Shang-Chi decisively beat Moving Shadow, claiming his enemy's moves were, like his name, merely a lifeless shadow.

SHANG-CHI: MASTER OF KUNG FU #6 (APR. 2003) After defeating Saint Germain, Shang-Chi parted ways with Black Jack Tarr, Clive Reston, and Leiko. He returned to his island and resumed his life as a teacher.

Saint Germain had a simple plan: to destroy the world with his deadly "Hellfire" weapon that would create apocalyptic lightning storms across the world. With humanity all but destroyed, Saint Germain would set about repopulating the planet with his own brainwashed followers. After tracking down and rescuing Leiko, Shang-Chi teamed up with Reston and fellow agent Black Jack Tarr to track Saint Germain to his island base, located a 12-hour sea voyage from Hong Kong. However, another group of MI-6 operatives was after the same target. Morgan Spetz and his Omega Team were a ruthless squad of agents who would stop at nothing to achieve their goal of killing Saint Germain.

Shang-Chi, his allies, and the Omega Team infiltrated the Ghost's Hellfire base and sought to stop his insane plans. Spetz and his team were all but wiped out, with Shang-Chi once again facing Moving Shadow. Like Shang-Chi, his deadly adversary had been raised to be the perfect assassin. This time their fight was hard and merciless. Moving Shadow was younger and faster, but lacked Shang-Chi's experience. Shang-Chi defeated him, but refused to land the killing blow. Saint Germain had no such compunction and killed Moving Shadow, sickened by his failure. With his Hellfire weapon now primed and targeted on London, Saint Germain still believed his plan was succeeding. Unknown to him, however, Clive Reston and his allies—having failed to destroy the weapon—managed to change the target from London to Hellfire Island itself. Shang-Chi watched as Saint Germain plunged to his doom and the island was destroyed. Shang-Chi left with his allies, returning to his own island home where he once again tried to find the peace he so craved: achieving a balance between light and shadow.

HEROES FOR HIRE #9 (JUN. 2007) As part of Misty Knight and Colleen Wing's Heroes for Hire team, Shang-Chi met Maria Vasquez (aka Tarantula), a Latina hero skilled in Gracie jiu-jitsu and mixed martial arts.

Heroes and Dragons

When Shang-Chi's ally and friend Iron Fist formed his own Heroes for Hire team, he recruited heroes depending on the needs of the individual mission.

When tasked with retrieving an ancient statue of the famous Chinese warrior Mulan, Shang-Chi was one of those Iron Fist turned to for help, along with swordswoman Colleen Wing and Shen Kuei, the Cat. The statue had been taken by a pirate called

UH, WE'RE THE "HEROES FOR HIRE"? WE'RE HERE ABOUT A JOB?

Lionmane and was tracked to Madripoor, an island in Southeast Asia, where it was due to be auctioned. The statue was destroyed when rogue Chinese General Lo Chien attacked the auction house. Shang-Chi and his allies suspected the general and Lionmane might actually be one and the same. It transpired that Lionmane was using piracy to increase his wealth, while his role as a general helped boost his standing in China. Assisted by the mutant Wolverine and Jessica Drew (Spider-Woman), Shang-Chi and his allies stopped the general's plans and learned that the Cat had secretly been working for the villain.

Later, Shang-Chi became involved in a different incarnation of Heroes for Hire. This team, created by Misty Knight and Colleen Wing, was set up

following the Stamford Incident—when Super Heroes were forced to give their secret identities to the US government, or face arrest. Being part of the team saw Shang-Chi go through a troubling time, losing the balance and serenity he had spent his life developing.

When a villainous quartet known as the Headmen kidnapped his ally Humbug, and a Doombot working with them killed his teammate Orka, Shang-Chi tore through the villains, defeating them in a maelstrom of kung fu. As team member Tarantula (Maria Vasquez), bandaged Shang-Chi's damaged hands, he felt attraction for her, even though he was appalled by her love of violence. It was an attraction that Shang-Chi gave in to when Heroes for Hire were sent to the remote Savage Land to find the prehistoric Moon-Boy.

Upon the team's return, they found themselves caught up in the middle of Hulk's attack on the world, after he returned from being banished into space. When Tarantula and Colleen were captured by aliens brought to Earth by the Hulk, Shang-Chi helped free them, only to discover Humbug had fallen under the control of a Brood Queen and been mutated into an incubator for her eggs. Shang-Chi also learned that Humbug had been responsible for Tarantula and Colleen's capture. Angered by Humbug's actions and for what his friend had been transformed into, Shang-Chi snapped his neck. The team split and Shang-Chi left with an injured Tarantula. Eventually the pair separated, as Shang-Chi sought to restore his balance.

Above: HEROES FOR HIRE #8 (MAY. 2007) Following his teammate Orka's death and a ferocious assault on the Headmen, Shang-Chi turned the Doombot's deathray back on itself, destroying it.

Right: HEROES FOR HIRE #9 (JUN. 2007) After Tarantula slaughtered some prehistoric beasts attacking them, Shang-Chi gave in to the intense attraction he felt for his teammate.

Below: HEROES FOR HIRE #15 (DEC. 2007) Despite the pleas of his teammates, Shang-Chi returned to the center of the Brood's hive to face Humbug. Seeing what his friend had become, Shang-Chi ended his life.

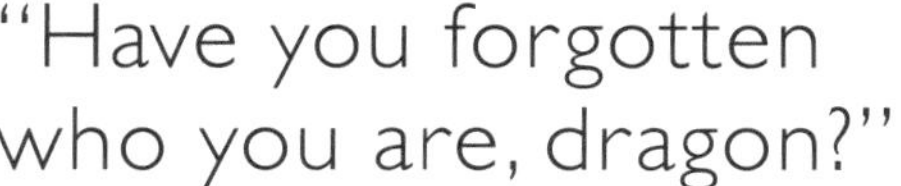

"Have you forgotten who you are, dragon?"

SHANG-CHI

Shang-Chi returned to action when an MI-13 operative asked for his help. Pete Wisdom was tracking a dragon in Cardiff, Wales. Not just any dragon, but the Welsh dragon that was the symbol of the nation. It wasn't a myth, it was real and had seen better days. The dragon had taken on the form of a Welsh gangster named Dave Griffin and lost itself in the process. To draw out the dragon, Wisdom used an ancient rite to challenge the gangster, before declaring that Shang-Chi would be his noble champion for the ensuing fight.

Shang-Chi desired to free the dragon from its mortal bonds and, sure enough, angered after a few rounds with Shang-Chi, Griffin started to siphon energy from those in the local area and returned to his dragon form. As they fought, Shang-Chi explained that he didn't fight to win, but merely show the dragon the fullness of its existence. The dragon declared it was too late for redemption and hurled Shang-Chi into the sky—but rather than let the hero fall to his death, it chose to save him by shielding Shang-Chi's body from the impact of his fall. This expense of energy returned the dragon to human form.

In the aftermath, Shang-Chi reminded Wisdom that he had promised the dragon its freedom, but Wisdom had lied; Griffin was handcuffed and led away. Shang-Chi then departed, saying that he couldn't sympathize with a man who was engineering his own karmic downfall.

Opposite and Left: WISDOM #3 (APR. 2007) Dave Griffin was the criminal kingpin of Wales. Entering Griffin's pub hangout, Shang-Chi defeated his thugs with ease, then used his kung fu to remind Griffin of his true, ancient nature.

"From this point on, you shall learn the Way of the Spider!"

SHANG-CHI

Opposite: FREE COMIC BOOK DAY: THE AMAZING SPIDER-MAN (MAY 2011) Zheng Zu had once trained Hai-Dai assassins in his now abandoned base. Shang-Chi trained Spider-Man there, hoping it would restore balance to the compound.

Below: SPIDER ISLAND: DEADLY HANDS OF KUNG FU #1 (OCT. 2011) Using a dance-like sequence of kung fu moves, Shang-Chi joined the fight against the spider-empowered troublemakers.

Way of the Spider

When Spider-Man lost his spider-sense, Shang-Chi stepped in to help his old friend. The web-slinger became his student and learned his own version of kung fu—the Way of the Spider or, as Spider-Man called it, "spider-fu."

Shang-Chi met his new student at one of Zheng Zu's abandoned bases. He explained that kung fu wasn't just about learning a set of movements—it was about turning what you learned into an art, about making it part of you. After teaching Spider-Man the basics—placing a power-dampener collar on the wall-crawler so he couldn't use his spider-powers while training—Shang-Chi showed Peter Parker how to use his new skills to create his own fighting style: the Way of the Spider.

The training was just in time, for the web-slinger soon had to face one of his greatest threats: the Jackal. The biochemistry professor-turned-villain was using genetically engineered bedbugs to imbue the population of Manhattan with spider-powers (and eventually mutate them into giant spiders, giving the Spider-Queen—an irradiated ex-marine named Adriana Soria—more power).

Even Shang-Chi found he had been affected. He had also been having nightmares of Fat Cobra (one of the Immortal Weapons, allies of the Iron Fist, Danny Rand) cocooned in webbing. He turned to clairvoyant Madame Web for advice, only to receive a cryptic answer from her that his future was uncertain and full of darkness and confusion. Before Shang-Chi could learn more, he went into battle to aid Iron Fist—who was facing off against a gang of spider-powered New Yorkers who were running amok. When the pair were joined by Rand's erstwhile ally the Bride of Nine Spiders, Shang-Chi was surprised when the two abruptly left with the fight still raging. Shang-Chi followed—only to see the Bride placing Iron Fist in a cocoon.

Shang-Chi leapt to Iron Fist's aid, fighting the Bride and defeating her. But rather than landing a final blow, he made the mistake of holding back—allowing the Bride to renew her attack and surprise Shang-Chi with a vicious kick, rendering him unconscious. As he lay motionless, the Bride made off with the cocooned Iron Fist, stating that he would make a good meal for her new master.

Shang-Chi was helped back home by fellow martial artist Silver Sable. After recovering, he tracked the Bride to an old mansion in Manhattan. Inside, Shang-Chi realized that it was the Bride herself who had sent out the visions he'd been having. She had fallen under the Spider-Queen's control, but part of her remained free and had sent out a telepathic warning to her allies. After Shang-Chi freed Iron Fist from his cocoon, the two heroes defeated the Bride. Then, overcome by the spider plague, Shang-Chi passed out just as their true enemy appeared.

Ai Apaec was a villainous Spider-God once used by Norman Osborn as one of his Dark Avengers. As Iron Fist prepared to fight the powerful chimera, he was rejoined by a now-conscious Shang-Chi. Undergoing the next step of the spider-mutation, Shang-Chi had grown four extra arms, but his mental training allowed him to fight a full transformation into a giant spider. While Iron Fist freed his fellow Immortal Weapons, Shang-Chi fought Ai Apaec, but all the while he could sense the change growing stronger—even his cast-iron will was having trouble holding back the Spider-Queen's influence. As he mutated further, he refused to surrender his humanity. Luckily, Iron Fist used his chi energy to finally rid Shang-Chi of the Jackal's spider virus.

Shang-Chi urged the Immortal Weapons to leave and help others in Manhattan—promising to deal with Ai Apaec himself. The godlike being mocked Shang-Chi, but now, fully restored to peak health and fitness, the martial arts master used his skill and intelligence against his eight-legged foe and brought the mansion down onto Ai Apaec, killing him. Leaving the rubble, Shang-Chi rejoined his fellow martial artists to help Spider-Man finally defeat the Jackal and the Spider-Queen.

Opposite and Above: SPIDER ISLAND: DEADLY HANDS OF KUNG FU #2 (NOV. 2011) Shang-Chi's visions of the Bride of Nine Spiders helped Silver Sable locate her lair. As Shang-Chi sought to help his cocooned friends, his body started to change.

SPIDER ISLAND: DEADLY HANDS OF KUNG FU #3 (DEC. 2011) A reinvigorated Shang-Chi brought the house down on Ai Apaec with a powerful Thunder Kick.

Avengers Assemble!

When Steve Rogers (at the time head of intelligence agency S.H.I.E.L.D.) formed a covert group of Super Heroes dubbed the Secret Avengers, he found himself at war with a powerful group of mercenaries and businessmen—the Shadow Council—who sought world domination.

Desiring to gain more power in China, the Shadow Council tried to raise an ancient Chinese sorcerer from the dead to join their ranks, but soon realized to complete the process they would need the life force of his son: Shang-Chi.

Shang-Chi guessed his father was trying to return when he was attacked by Hai-Dai, a group of his father's ninja-like warriors. He managed to defeat them with the help of the mysterious Prince of Orphans, a legendary martial artist who was an ally of both Iron Fist and Steve Rogers. Shang-Chi soon learned that the Shadow Council were seeking the "Eyes of the Dragon," a powerful amulet that could bring someone back to life. Legends said that two sorcerers had used the amulet centuries before, pouring the last of their life forces into it. Team member Beast discovered that one of these sorcerers was Shang-Chi's father and had been called Zheng Zu. When the Secret Avengers traveled to Hong Kong looking for two rubies linked to the amulet, they walked straight into a trap. The Shadow Council weren't just planning to resurrect Shang-Chi's father—they had already begun the process and needed Shang-Chi to complete it.

The Secret Avengers heard reports that Zheng Zu had unleashed a terrorist attack on downtown Hong Kong and rushed to the scene to stop him. However, Shang-Chi sensed something was amiss. The attack was a distraction that allowed Shadow Council agents to capture Sharon Carter, Captain America's lover. With Carter now their prisoner, the Shadow Council offered Steve Rogers a deal—Shang-Chi for the woman he loved. The martial arts master allowed a

SECRET AVENGERS #6 (DEC. 2010) Shang-Chi sensed that his father was alive again moments before an attack by the deadly Hai-Dai.

swap to take place and learned that while his father had indeed returned from the grave, he still wasn't complete; Zheng Zu needed to conduct an ancient ceremony using the Eyes of the Dragon amulet to steal his son's life force and fully return.

As the ceremony started, one of the Shadow Council's agents was revealed to be Moon Knight, undercover. He was soon joined by his fellow Secret Avengers, but with Shang-Chi hanging bound and helpless like a lamb to the slaughter, it seemed the ceremony would be successful and his allies too late. Having been cut by his father, Shang-Chi's blood was already starting to flow and Zheng Zu's strength beginning to increase. Fortunately, the Prince of Orphans was on hand to destroy Zheng Zu before the sorcerer's body could be fully restored. The Shadow Council hastily retreated and Shang-Chi was safe. As he departed, he told Steve Rogers that he was in his debt and would always be there when required.

SECRET AVENGERS #9 (MAR. 2011) Zheng Zu had only been partially reborn, his body still skeletal. He required his son's blood to finish the ancient rites of rebirth.

Right: AVENGERS #11 (JUL. 2013) Shang-Chi's new electrified nunchaku helped him defeat A.I.M. assassins while on a mission for the Avengers.

SECRET AVENGERS #18 (DEC. 2011) The Shadow Council's "No Zone" was a special base taken from another dimension where the normal rules of time and space did not apply, making the Avengers' mission even more dangerous.

It wasn't long before Steve Rogers called on Shang-Chi for his assistance. When Rogers learned of a Shadow Council base that was using a dangerous element called Transmatter (taken from the Negative Zone) to build a doomsday device, he employed Shang-Chi and Sharon Carter to help him infiltrate the base. Shang-Chi soon grew to resent being turned into Rogers' thug, having to use his skills to take down the base's many agents. However, Shang-Chi's skills helped them locate the flight deck where they found the base was under the command of tech genius Arnim Zola 4.2.3, an updated version of Rogers' old enemy. Zola escaped with the doomsday device on a special craft, but Rogers also managed to board and Zola was no match for his old foe. The Transmatter was secured and for Shang-Chi, it was a debt paid. He had also proven to be a valuable member of the team, so when Captain America and Iron Man later formed a larger Avengers task force, Shang-Chi was one of the first names on their list.

Shang-Chi saw his role as an Avenger as a chance to test himself like never before. To help against some of the more cosmic foes Shang-Chi would face, Tony Stark made him a pair of gauntlets that could project his energy and a set of nunchaku that could be electrified. As part of the team, Shang-Chi faced alien threats such as the Builders and helped defend the Earth from Mad Titan Thanos' legions. Fighting as part of such a large group against these cosmic foes was a new experience for Shang-Chi. His training often helped him achieve things where more powerful Avengers had failed—such as persuading a new Captain Universe to open up about a danger that threatened all reality.

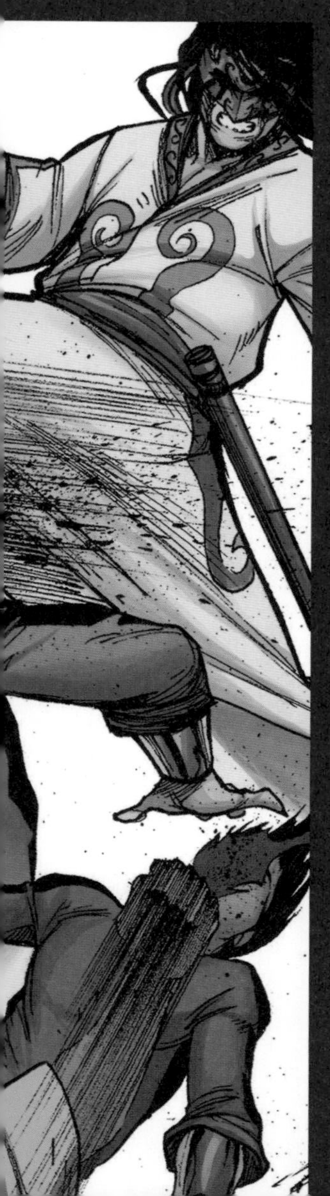

One of the stranger moments in Shang-Chi's time as an Avenger occurred after one of his rare defeats. He was part of a small team of Avengers sent to investigate trouble in the Southeast Asian island of Madripoor, along with Falcon, Black Widow, and Wolverine. Shang-Chi soon learned that the martial arts master and mutant known as Gorgon had taken over the ninja clan called the Hand, and was trying to conduct an ancient rite that would wake the giant dragon upon which Madripoor was built. Shang-Chi found the Hand's temple home and faced Gorgon. He was too late. The rite had already taken place and the city of Madripoor was now in the sky—the dragon beneath it having taken flight under Gorgon's control. Shang-Chi battled Gorgon and lost: the super-powered killer was too much for him. Once defeated, Shang-Chi was thrown off the dragon's side.

Shang-Chi's body was found and healed by S.P.E.A.R., China's answer to S.H.I.E.L.D. With their help, he soon returned to action—this time fueled by size-altering Pym Particles, courtesy of the Avengers. Shang-Chi grew to giant size to face the dragon which was causing chaos and destruction in Shanghai. The giant-size Shang-Chi dealt with Gorgon and the Hand by casually flicking their temple from the dragon's head and then landed a knock-out blow on the dragon itself.

Left and below left: AVENGERS WORLD #3 (APR. 2014) While Shang-Chi easily defeated Gorgon's Hand assassins, he knew he was no match for their leader. It was to his credit that he fought anyway, and managed to wound the powerful mutant.

While a giant-size Shang-Chi was only a brief transformation, he gained a new ability when investigating the events known as "Incursions." Captain Universe's earlier warning was becoming all too real; Earths from other realities were being destroyed and Shang-Chi's home was seemingly doomed as ancient beings called the Beyonders started wiping out entire universes.

Shang-Chi was sent to Kobe, Japan, to investigate a genetic "Origin Bomb" that had gone off, signaling the start of Earth's destruction. Shang-Chi bonded with the alien technology and the city's mutated residents, gaining the ability to create multiple replicas of himself. His new super-powers did not last long, however. Shortly after, reality itself was destroyed and remade following the fight against the Beyonders. A new version of Earth came into existence in the aftermath, one where Shang-Chi was human again, his super-powers seemingly no more. While Shang-Chi's time as an Avenger was coming to an end, he would soon join another super-powered group—albeit under very strange circumstances.

Below: AVENGERS WORLD #14 (DEC. 2014) Growing to immense size thanks to the Pym Particles he had been given, Shang-Chi faced the Madripoor dragon on more equal terms.

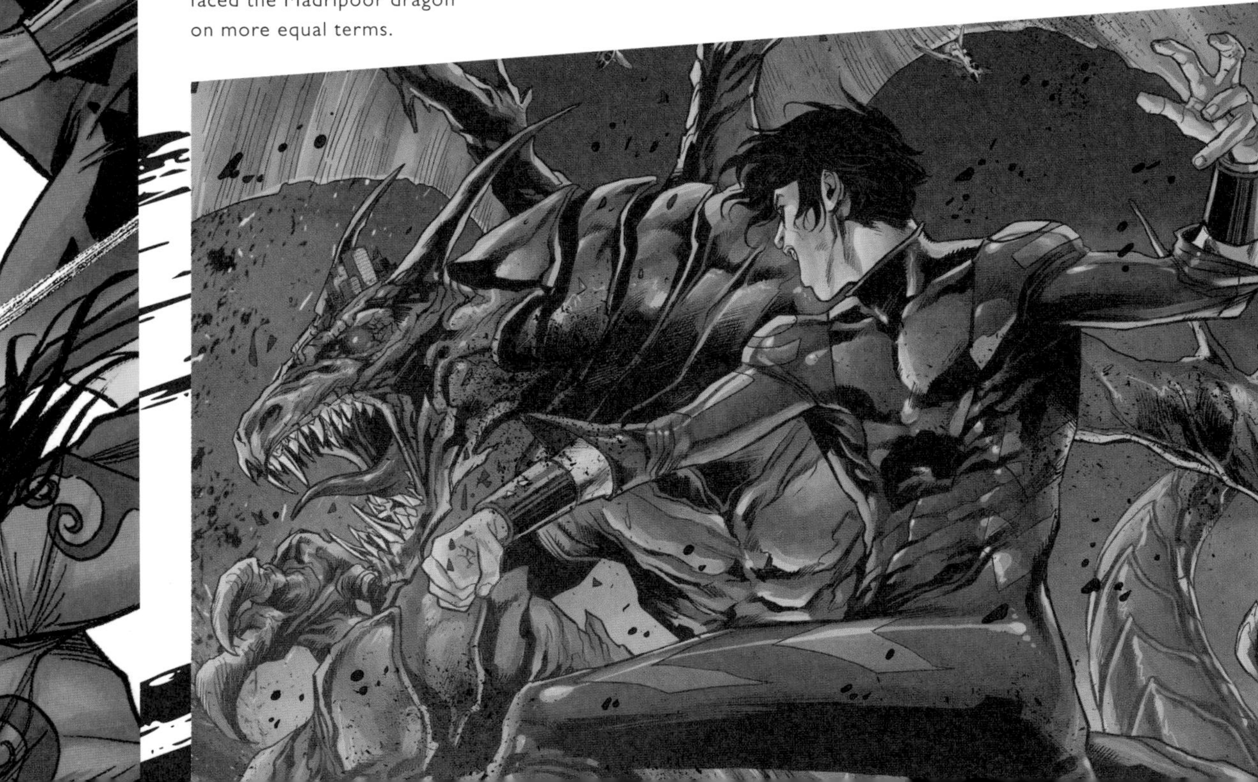

War and Peace

Following his time in the Avengers, Shang-Chi went back to concentrating on his training and helping those in need.

One of the causes he supported was a New York benefit to encourage Asian-American bone marrow donation, where he appeared alongside Ms. Marvel (Kamala Khan), Amadeus Cho (the Hulk), Jake Oh (an agent of S.H.I.E.L.D.), Silk (Cindy Moon), and Jimmy Woo (leader of the Agents of Atlas). In the aftermath, Shang-Chi found himself part of a new team: the Protectors.

The team came about by accident; Shang-Chi took his friends to a karaoke club after their appearance at the benefit, but just as their night was about to end, aliens from the planet Seknark Seven attacked. Led by Prince Regent Phalkan, the aliens wanted humans for food—and thought the best way was to take a big chunk of Manhattan and its inhabitants back to their homeworld. Once in space, trapped on the piece of Manhattan, Shang-Chi helped everyone overcome the Prince and defeat the aliens, before galactic defense team Alpha Flight arrived to clean up and take everyone home.

Opposite: NEW AGENTS OF ATLAS #1 (JUL. 2019) Shang-Chi alongside his Agents of Atlas teammates: Amadeus Cho (now calling himself Brawn), Aero, Crescent and Io, Jimmy Woo, Luna Snow, Sword Master, Silk, and White Fox.

TOTALLY AWESOME HULK #15 (MAR. 2017) After bonding over a Korean meal, Shang-Chi and his new friends went to karaoke, Shang-Chi leading the way with a rendition of "New York, New York!"

TOTALLY AWESOME HULK #16 (APR. 2017) Shang-Chi's training and focus made him more than a match for the alien invaders.

BAD REPUTATION.
BAD
BAD

"Magic means nothing... power means nothing... without skill."

SHANG-CHI

On his return to Earth, Shang-Chi spent time in Hong Kong, where mutant mercenary Domino tracked him down and asked for his help. She was having trouble controlling her powers and hoped Shang-Chi could train her. He agreed to help her calm the damage to her chi. Domino had an instant crush on the martial arts master and was in awe of his combat skills. When the pair took a night off training to go dancing in a Kowloon nightclub, they were attacked by a group of Shang-Chi's enemies, including Razor Fist and a resurrected Midnight Sun. Shang-Chi showed Domino a way to regain control of her luck powers and use the ability to defeat her opponents. With the threat at an end, the master and student seemed to be growing closer. That changed when Shang-Chi helped Domino fight one of her foes, Topaz. With the villain defeated, Shang-Chi witnessed the savage side of Domino when she executed her enemy. The act represented everything Shang-Chi opposed and he told Domino that she could no longer be his student.

Shang-Chi was soon fighting alongside the Protectors again, although the team gained a new name. Jimmy Woo was already considering using them as a new incarnation of his Agents of Atlas team when the Dark Elf Malekith brought his "War of the Realms" to Earth, sending Dark Elves and Fire Demons to conquer the world. Shang-Chi joined his friends to help those in Asia fight Malekith's ally, a Fire Giant called the Queen of Cinders.

During the chaotic struggle, Shang-Chi met teenager Lin Lie who also went by the name of Sword Master. Shang-Chi was impressed with the teenager and his sword, but told him he needed further training. After helping defend Shanghai, the team spent a night preparing to take the fight to the Queen of Cinders. Woo tasked Shang-Chi with training the new heroes to fight better, both individually and as a team. As they rejoined the battle, they worked far better together and—thanks to Shang-Chi's training and Chinese hero Monkey King sacrificing himself in battle—defeated the Queen. For Woo, it was proof that he had a strong new team to work with, and one in which Shang-Chi was an essential part: the new Agents of Atlas.

Opposite and above: DOMINO #4 (SEP. 2018) An initially frustrated Shang-Chi told Domino to take her training more seriously. Though he soon felt an attraction to his new student.

Shang-Chi soon took on Lin Lie as a student. When Sword Master moved to New York in search of his missing father, Shang-Chi was on hand to help. Shang-Chi again pointed out that Lie didn't know how to use his skills properly and Lie was eventually forced to admit Shang-Chi was right. Lie was a troublesome student and Shang-Chi was concerned about nightmares he was having in which his student killed him. It made Shang-Chi realize that Lie had to learn how to control both his temper and his sword.

After only a few training sessions, Ares the God of War appeared and tried to steal Lie's sword. When Shang-Chi tracked him down, Ares claimed he needed the sword to kill a god—one who had kidnapped his son, Ismenios. A brief skirmish followed, but Shang-Chi held his own against the God of War, before agreeing to help him. The three traveled to the island nation of Madripoor and confronted Davi Naka, Madripoor's mother goddess, who had Ismenios imprisoned in her realm. Shang-Chi learned that Davi hadn't kidnapped Ismenios, but instead saved his life when he had tried to steal treasure from Atlantis after the kingdom's guardian dragon had gone missing. Davi warned the heroes that Prince Namor would be out for revenge.

With the help of the Agents of Atlas, Shang-Chi learned that tech wiz Mike Nguyen, CEO of the Big Nguyen Company, had created a "portal city" called Pan—its portals linked many of the world's cities into a single metropolis. The portals were powered by the scales of captured dragons, including the dragon taken from Atlantis. It looked like there would be a war between Atlantis and the new city, with Shang-Chi and his allies caught in the middle. Eventually, after helping to save Pan, Shang-Chi realized he had been caught up in yet another game of death and deceit and left the Agents of Atlas, seeking to find his own path once again.

SWORD MASTER #5 (JAN. 2020) Shang-Chi and Sword Master fought Golems after entering Davi Naka's temple, with Shang-Chi using the encounter to teach his student an important lesson.

ATLANTIS ATTACKS #2 (APR. 2020) Shang-Chi and his allies defended Pan from an enraged Namor—little realizing they had been caught up in Mike Nguyen's dangerous plans.

SHANG-CHI #2 OCT. 2020) As Zheng Zu raged at his children for sneaking into his forbidden laboratory, Shang-Chi's sister leaped to her brother's defense.

Brothers and Sisters

Shang-Chi had finally found a refuge from his turbulent, action-packed life. He was working in Grandma Wang's bakery in San Francisco's Chinatown, living a quiet life above her shop.

The peace didn't last long. His old ally Leiko Wu arrived to warn him that his father's organization was active again. When Shang-Chi and Leiko were ambushed shortly afterward, they were aided by two warriors who introduced themselves as Brother Sabre and Sister Dagger. Shang-Chi learned that his father had created a group called the Five Weapons Society centuries earlier in China, and the Hunan compound where Shang-Chi had been raised was actually the House of the Deadly Hand, one of its five headquarters. The other houses were Staff, Dagger, Hammer, and Sabre, each led by a "Brother" or "Sister." Brother Sabre and Sister Dagger had opposed Sister Hammer when she had decided to take over as leader of the Five Weapons Society even though Zheng Zhu's spirit had apparently chosen Shang-Chi to do so. When Shang-Chi learned that Sister Hammer had a strange tattoo on her forehead he realized she must be his long-lost sister, Shi-Hua. She had been the only other child of Shang-Chi's mother and Zheng Zu. When they were both young, Shang-Chi and Shi-Hua had discovered their father's secret laboratory where Zheng Zu was conducting experiments to reanimate corpses. After Zheng Zu threatened the young Shang-Chi, his sister attacked their father. Zheng Zu was about to kill his daughter when Shang-Chi begged their father to grant her mercy. Zheng Zu agreed and Shang-Chi never saw his sister again. He believed his father had

Opposite above: SHANG-CHI #2 OCT. 2020) Shi-Hua had been transformed into the mighty Sister Hammer. Her enormous strength made her a devastating foe in close combat.

mercifully granted her a quick death, but now he learned that she had been moved to another location—the House of the Deadly Hammer in Russia, where she had spent years training. She now sought to remake the world in their father's image.

Shang-Chi tracked her down to the House of the Deadly Staff outside London—his sister had already killed Brother Staff and taken over his headquarters. He was met with a friendly meal, the two sharing memories of better times. However, Sister Hammer had poisoned her brother. He passed out and woke in her lab, where scientists were creating Jiangshi: undead, vampire-like creatures.

As Shang-Chi tried to fight his way out of the lab, he was helped by the sudden appearance of Sister Dagger and Brother Sabre. The three managed to escape—though Shang-Chi was wounded in the fight with the Jiangshi.

At Sister Dagger's Parisian base, Shang-Chi started to see visions of a skeletal ghost he believed to be his father. The spirit led him to the shrine room of Sister Dagger's house and revealed another, hidden room—the spirit's shrine. It transpired that it wasn't his father's ghost but that of his uncle, Zheng Yi. The ghost also revealed a map that led to his tomb. Shang-Chi turned to Leiko for help, and she used MI-6's satellites to provide Shang-Chi with a location for his uncle's resting place. Leiko also warned him that MI-5 was about to launch a full-scale assault on his new "family" and their houses, and that Sister Hammer and her warriors had broken into the Chinese exhibit at the Louvre. Shang-Chi and his allies raced to intervene, but his sister escaped.

Right: SHANG-CHI #3 NOV. 2020) Shang-Chi found himself guided by the spirit of his uncle, Zheng Yi. He realized that the key to defeating his sister must lie in Zheng Yi's tomb.

Brother Sabre and Sister Dagger traveled with Shang-Chi to his uncle's tomb, high in the mountains of Hunan Provence in China. They soon found themselves facing a deadly creature left to guard the tomb. Dagger and Sabre urged Shang-Chi to travel on while they fought the creature. When Shang-Chi entered the burial chamber, Zheng Yi appeared and revealed the truth about his death. Shang-Chi had been led to believe that Zheng Zu had killed his brother using the Eyes of the Dragon to gain eternal life. The truth was that his uncle had willingly given his life so Zheng Zu would live on to continue their work protecting China. Unfortunately, without his younger brother for balance, Zheng Zu took a darker path. When Shang-Chi asked if his uncle could heal his wounds, Zheng Yi told him he would need to find peace with himself and his family for the wounds to heal.

Sister Hammer, meanwhile, had progressed with her plan. MI-5 attacked the House of the Deadly Staff, but she had laid a trap for them—she wanted to use their bodies to create a Jiangshi army. Shang-Chi, Sister Dagger, and Brother Sabre joined forces with Leiko and MI-6 to try and stop Sister Hammer's undead army as it launched a full-scale assault on London. Shang-Chi confronted his sister and, using the knowledge passed to him by Zheng Yi, managed to break her connection with her Jiangshi warriors. She was shot and killed in the fighting by an MI-6 operative. The threat was at an end. In the aftermath, Shang-Chi decided to accept his role as Supreme Commander of the Five Houses, hoping to use them as a force for good in the world. However, it was also possible that he would turn to darkness and follow in his father's footsteps...

SHANG-CHI #5 (JAN. 2021) Alongside his new allies Sister Dagger and Brother Sabre, Shang-Chi ended his long-lost sister's bid for power.

"Just as the body is governed by its mind, so does the mind rely on the body."

SHANG-CHI

IRON FIST

THE LIVING WEAPON

Danny Rand is Iron Fist, the legendary protector of the mystical city of K'un-Lun. Danny isn't the first to attain the mantle—66 noble warriors have preceded him, each besting the deadly dragon Shou-Lao in combat, and then plunging their fists into the dragon's melted heart to gain its energy. The first Iron Fist left K'un-Lun in 1,000,000BCE, while others have fought Mongol hordes, walked the trail in the Wild West, and faced the horrors of World War I. Many have died young, hunted by a demon who feeds off their powerful chi, killing them when they turn 33 years of age. Danny is one of the few to live beyond that age and, while he first wanted to use his skills to avenge the death of his father, he has gone on to become a true hero. He has faced the likes of the mutant Sabretooth, sorcerer Master Khan, and master martial artist the Steel Serpent, while also fighting as part of teams such as the Defenders and the Avengers. Perhaps he is best known for his work alongside Luke Cage as Heroes for Hire, bringing justice to the streets of New York City and beyond.

Since becoming the latest warrior to don the mantle of Iron Fist, Danny has learned the dark truth about K'un-Lun, fought as its champion in a cosmic tournament of mystical cities, and aided a revolution. Danny Rand doesn't just protect K'un-Lun, he protects the noble ideals of what K'un-Lun should be. He is one of the deadliest martial artists in the world, whose power and skills rival even those of Shang-Chi. No wonder some call him the Living Weapon.

IMMORTAL IRON FIST #1 (JAN. 2007)
Danny Rand is the latest warrior to become Iron Fist, a kung fu master powered by the chi of the immortal dragon, Shou-Lao, making his fists "like unto a thing of iron."

Protector of K'un-Lun

The mystical city of K'un-Lun was created by humanoid extraterrestrials when their spaceship crash-landed into the Himalayan mountains.

The impact of the vessel's engines caused the craft to enter a pocket dimension, separating it and the land around it from the rest of Earth, only permitting travel between the two at certain times. The survivors built the city from the remains of their ship, its name inspiring the name of the surrounding Kunlun mountains. However, the settlers were not the only inhabitants of the pocket dimension. A vicious plantlike race called the H'ylthri were its original residents and they have spent lifetimes trying to kill the invaders, sometimes taking on human form to infiltrate K'un-Lun in attempts to bring about its destruction from within. The area was also home to powerful dragons, with Shou-Lao the greatest of them.

K'un-Lun was ruled by the Dragon-Kings, powerful sorcerers who could manifest in human or dragon form. Their leader, bestowed with the title Yu-Ti, spoke on their behalf. In the city's distant past the Dragon-Kings fell under the influence of an evil sorcerer known as Master Khan, who they came to worship as a god.

K'un-Lun has always taught its inhabitants martial arts, with the best being tutored by Lei-Kung the Thunderer, one of the many immortals living in the city.

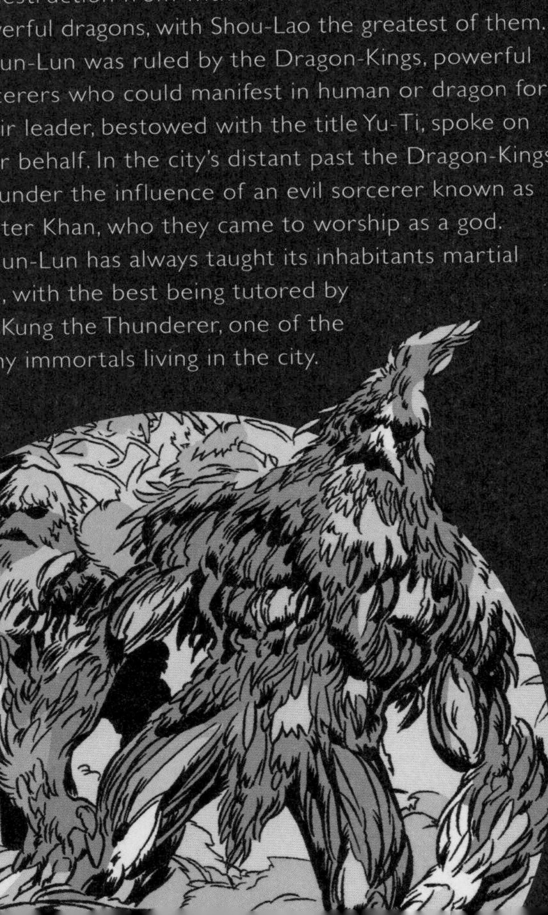

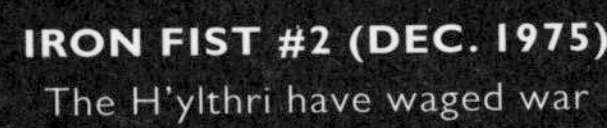

IRON FIST #2 (DEC. 1975)
The H'ylthri have waged war on K'un-Lun for millennia, using their human captives as food for their young.

AVENGERS #13 (MAR. 2019) K'un-Lun is one of the Seven Capital Cities of Heaven that occasionally connect with Earth. The other cities are K'un-Zi, Peng Lai Island, Z'Gambo, Kingdom of Spiders, Under City, and Tiger Island.

The first warrior to be called Iron Fist was a young girl named Fan Fei, who lived in 1,000,000 BCE. Raised in K'un-Lun, she had mastered the art of kung fu and secretly began teaching it to the cavemen struggling to survive beyond K'un-Lun's walls. When K'un-Lun's rulers heard of her actions, they forced her to watch as the city's sacred dragon, Shou-Lao, executed them. In a rage, the 15-year-old Fan Fei attacked and punched the dragon, killing it. The act left her with a dragon-like scar on the back of her right hand and the power of the dragon's chi. For her crime she was exiled from K'un-Lun and as she left, Lei-Kung the Thunderer told her to take her foul "iron fists" with her.

Fan Fei roamed the ancient land, aiding primitive humans against threats such as Gorgilla the Gorilla King and his gorilla legions. She also met with the demon Mephisto, ignoring his attempts to win her over to his side. In time, her path led her back to K'un-Lun, where Lei-Kung revealed to Fan Fei that Shou-Lao had been reborn and was, in fact, immortal. The Dragon-Kings had been impressed with Fan Fei and wanted her to return and become the city's protector. She refused and decided to remain on Earth, eventually joining an early incarnation of the Avengers with heroes Odin, Agamotto, Phoenix, Black Panther, Starbrand, and Ghost Rider. They fought powerful entities, including a Celestial—an ancient and nearly omnipotent entity.

AVENGERS #13 (MAR. 2019) When Fan Fei saw her students being killed by Shou-Lao, she broke free from her captors. She killed Shou-Lao with a Double Hammer Fist of Exquisite Doom, becoming the first to gain the power of the dragon's chi.

IMMORTAL IRON FIST #7 (AUG. 2007) Wu Ao-Shi was caught stealing as a young girl but saved from punishment by Lei-Kung, the Thunderer, who set her on the path to becoming Iron Fist.

Others who have assumed the Iron Fist name include Wu Ao-Shi, who left K'un-Lun to find her lover and eventually became a Pirate Queen; and a pacifist named Li Park who, in 730CE, became Iron Fist after a plague had decimated K'un-Lun. He left the city and helped save villagers from attacking hordes, bringing them back to K'un-Lun to live in peace. In the 15th century, Fongji Wu was another woman who took on the mantle of Iron Fist. She protected K'un-Lun from the Phoenix Force, merging with the powerful cosmic entity before departing for space.

Many of the Iron Fists died at the age of 33—killed by a demon known as Ch'i-Lin who hunted them for their chi energy. At the dawn of the 20th century, Orson Randall was born in K'un-Lun after his parents' airship crashed in the city. He learned the city's ways and eventually became Iron Fist. He later returned to Earth, fighting in World War I, and was one of the few Iron Fists to live beyond 33. He even took on a young ward, Wendell Rand, and filled his head with stories of the mystical city of K'un-Lun. Stories that would one day result in Wendell trying to seek out the city and his son, Danny Rand, adopting the mantle of Iron Fist.

IMMORTAL IRON FIST #15 (JUL. 2008) The Iron Fist Bei Bang-Wen fought against the British in the Second Opium War, then went on to team up with Indian hero Brahman in the 1860s to defeat the demonic Tiger Jani.

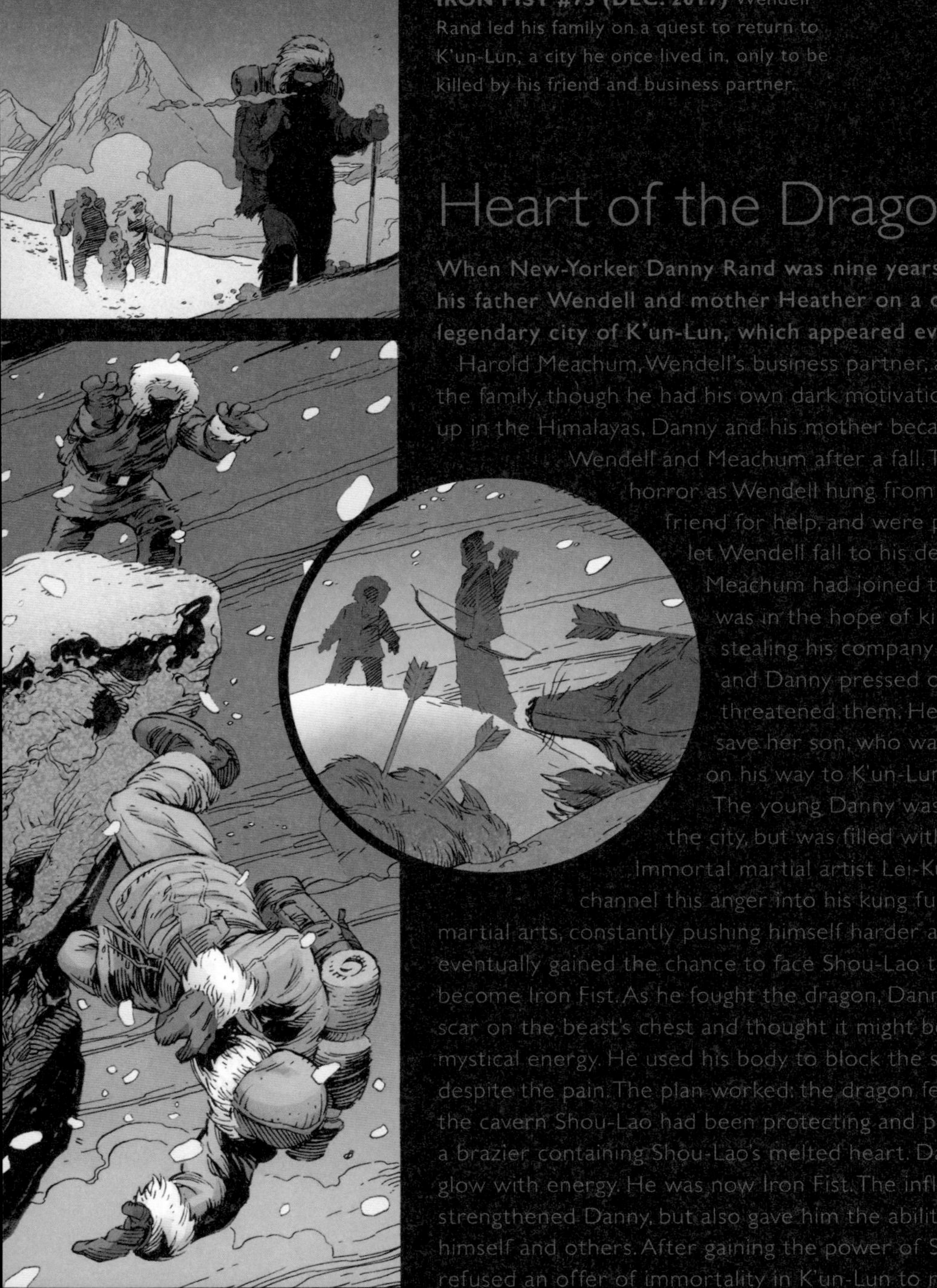

IRON FIST #73 (DEC. 2017) Wendell Rand led his family on a quest to return to K'un-Lun, a city he once lived in, only to be killed by his friend and business partner.

Heart of the Drago

When New-Yorker Danny Rand was nine years
his father Wendell and mother Heather on a c
legendary city of K'un-Lun, which appeared ev

Harold Meachum, Wendell's business partner, a
the family, though he had his own dark motivatio
up in the Himalayas, Danny and his mother beca
Wendell and Meachum after a fall. T
horror as Wendell hung from
friend for help, and were p
let Wendell fall to his de
Meachum had joined t
was in the hope of ki
stealing his company
and Danny pressed o
threatened them. He
save her son, who wa
on his way to K'un-Lun
The young Danny was
the city, but was filled with
Immortal martial artist Lei-Ku
channel this anger into his kung fu
martial arts, constantly pushing himself harder a
eventually gained the chance to face Shou-Lao t
become Iron Fist. As he fought the dragon, Danr
scar on the beast's chest and thought it might be
mystical energy. He used his body to block the s
despite the pain. The plan worked: the dragon fe
the cavern Shou-Lao had been protecting and pl
a brazier containing Shou-Lao's melted heart. Da
glow with energy. He was now Iron Fist. The infl
strengthened Danny, but also gave him the abilit
himself and others. After gaining the power of S
refused an offer of immortality in K'un-Lun to

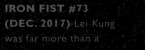

IRON FIST #73 (DEC. 2017) Lei-Kung was far more than a master to the young Danny Rand, in many ways he became his adoptive father.

Below: MARVEL PREMIERE: IRON FIST #16 (JUL. 1974) Many warriors had faced Shou-Lao the Undying. Not only was the dragon reborn after every death, it could breathe fire and move faster than lightning.

Below: IRON FIST #7 (SEP. 1976) Master Khan was a powerful sorcerer able to control the Crimson Bands of Cyttorak and the Flames of the Faltine.

NO TRICK, YOUNG DRAGON, YOU HAVE MY WORD OF HONOR ON THAT. THE PORTAL IS REALITY.
A DIMENSIONAL GATEWAY FROM EARTH TO K'UN-LUN.

Opposite: MARVEL TEAM-UP #63 (NOV. 1977) The Steel Serpent left Danny close to death after draining his chi. Fortunately Danny was able to reclaim his power.

Almost as soon as Danny arrived back in New York, he found himself under attack from assassins. Harold Meachum had spent the last decade preparing for Danny's return, as he had heard from a monk that Danny was in K'un-Lun and that the city's rulers believed he would become Iron Fist. When Danny finally confronted Meachum, he was shocked to discover a broken man. Danny's desire for vengeance left him and he let him live. However, when Meachum tried to shoot Danny in the back, a mysterious ninja appeared and killed the old man. Meachum's daughter, Joy, found Iron Fist standing near her father's corpse and alerted the police—making Iron Fist a wanted man. The mystery ninja had possessed the body of Lee Wing, father of Colleen Wing, a private investigator who had helped Danny. It transpired the ninja was a servant of Master Khan, a malign sorcerer who had once been worshiped as a god in K'un-Lun. Iron Fist was able to free Lee from the ninja's influence and prove his own innocence.

Iron Fist tracked down Khan and learned that his father, Wendell, had once been chosen as successor to K'un-Lun's ruler, Lord Tuan. Wendell had also nearly become the city's Iron Fist after defeating Davos—son of Lei-Kung—in single combat for the right to face Shou-Lao, but he turned his back on the role to return home. Davos had then tried to defeat Shou-Lao, but failed. As Davos had done so without permission, he had been exiled from K'un-Lun. Lord Tuan's son, Nu-An, took the throne and the title Yu-Ti upon his father's death, and had allowed Wendell and Heather Rand to die when they later tried to return.

Khan opened up a dimensional gateway to K'un-Lun, and offered Danny the chance to return and claim vengeance on Nu-An for betraying his father. Danny refused, destroying the gateway, which sucked Khan into its vortex as it closed.

In the ensuing months, Danny faced enemies such as the Wrecking Crew, Boomerang, and the mutant Sabretooth. He held his own against Wolverine and the X-Men when a mix-up led to conflict with the mutants. Davos, now calling himself Steel Serpent, attacked Danny twice—draining a little of his life force each time—before finally besting him in single combat. Davos drained his rival's chi to gain the full power of the Iron Fist. Danny's friend Misty Knight took the injured Danny to safety. Despite his weak state, Danny then faced Steel Serpent again. Davos tried to unleash the power of the Iron Fist during their fight, but it overloaded his body with energy. Danny was able to reclaim the power of Shou-Lao, and Davos seemingly died as the energy left him. Danny was Iron Fist once more… and about to meet a hero for hire who would become his closest friend.

SHKOW!

HE MAY HAVE A POINT, WHAT'S THE MAN MADE OF, ANYWAY? I HIT HIM WITH THE FULL FORCE OF THE IRON FIST--

HANDS LIKE VISE... CAN'T BREATHE...
BUT... I... SENSE AT HEART... POWER MAN ISN'T... KILLER.

Left: POWER MAN #48 (DEC. 1977) Iron Fist declared that striking Power Man was like hitting steel that wouldn't shatter. Luke's lack of fighting skill was more than made up for by his strength and rage.

POWER MAN & IRON FIST #50 (APR. 1978) Danny and Luke worked briefly for Knightwing Restorations before starting their own company, Heroes for Hire.

Heroes for Hire

While Luke Cage is Danny's best friend and brother-in-arms, it wasn't always that way: the first time they met, Luke nearly killed Danny.

Danny returned home after receiving a desperate call from his friend Colleen Wing: Power Man—Luke Cage—was attacking her. Danny and Colleen's best friend Misty Knight rushed to help, only for Misty to be knocked out by Cage. Iron Fist then stepped out of the shadows and punched Cage through the building's walls. Stunned, Luke considered it one of the hardest punches he'd ever taken. The two fought, but Danny sensed that Cage wasn't a killer. As Luke had his hands around Danny's throat, Danny took a chance and didn't fight back. The act brought Power Man to his senses. He apologized and told the trio that crime boss Bushmaster had sworn to kill two people close to him—Claire Temple and Dr. Noah Burstein—if Luke didn't bring him Misty Knight.

Framed for drug dealing, Cage had once been in jail at Seagate Penitentiary. He had escaped after illegal experiments had left him with super-strength and bulletproof skin. Danny and Misty helped Luke rescue his friends and defeat Bushmaster. Along the way, Danny and Luke developed a deep respect for each other, and gained a videotape that proved Cage was an innocent man. Forming "Heroes for Hire" they faced bad guys such as Hammerhead and Sabretooth.

"Iron Fist is finished... and you're next, Cage! 'Cause I got the power now!"

BUSHMASTER

Left: POWER MAN #49 (FEB. 1978) Bushmaster had forced Dr. Burstein to turn him into a new, stronger "Power Man."

Iron Fist's links with K'un-Lun placed both heroes in danger when they followed the ancient sorcerer Master Khan to K'un-Lun through a mystical portal. Danny was shocked to learn the plantlike H'ylthri were attacking K'un-Lun. Danny also began to understand more about his father's links to the city. Thirty years before, a young Wendell Rand had saved the previous ruler, Lord Tuan, and his son, Nu-An, from the dragon Shou-Lao. Injured, Wendell was taken to K'un-Lun and restored to health by a female healer called Shakirah, and adopted by Lord Tuan as his heir. Wendell married Shakirah and they had a child, Miranda, but Wendell turned his back on K'un-Lun when the H'ylthri killed his wife. Years later, Miranda fled K'un-Lun with her lover having been caught practicing kung fu—forbidden for a woman.

Danny and Luke joined the war against the H'ylthri, learning the green bipeds used living humans as fertilizer for their young—and had killed Danny's half-sister and her lover years before. As the rest of the city celebrated a victory over the H'ylthri, Danny was captured by Nu-An and offered up as a blood sacrifice to Master Khan—whom K'un-Lun's rulers regarded as a god. Much of Khan's power had come from warriors who had died fighting Shou-Lao and now he sought Iron Fist's power. Cage and the immortal martial artist Lei-Kung helped Danny escape. Before leaving the city, Danny shattered its Great Crystal, believing that he had severed the city's links to Earth.

When another confrontation between Iron Fist and Khan weakened the sorcerer, it gave a prisoner kept deep below the city a chance for freedom. Chiantang was a mighty Dragon-Lord who could take human form. According to K'un-Lun legend, Chiantang had turned a fisherman into Shou-Lao the Undying millennia before, after the fisherman had married and then shamed Chiantang's sister. Chiantang even tore out the creature's heart as extra punishment. When Danny had killed Shou-Lao—seemingly freeing the fisherman from his suffering—Chiantang had returned to K'un-Lun in a fury, only to be imprisoned by Master Khan. Years later, with Khan now

POWER MAN & IRON FIST #75 (NOV. 1981) On his return to K'un-Lun, then under attack by the H'ylthri, Iron Fist learned his father had been sent from the city into the world with the sole purpose of creating a perfect warrior—Danny—that Yu-Ti could one day sacrifice to Master Khan.

POWER MAN & IRON FIST #119 (SEP. 1985) Chiantang the Dragon-Lord had destroyed much of the city of K'un-Lun in Iron Fist's absence, and ruled the ruins through fear and terror.

weakened after a confrontation with Iron Fist, Chiantang broke free from his prison and rampaged through K'un-Lun in his dragon form. When Danny returned to K'un-Lun seeking a cure for radiation poisoning ravaging his body, he found the city destroyed. Luckily, Lei-Kung had survived and showed Danny how to heal himself. As Chiantang attacked them, Colleen Wing, Doctor Druid, Luke Cage, and Iron Fist joined Lei-Kung in a fight against the dragon, eventually opening a gateway to send Chiantang to the Netherworld.

With the threat to K'un-Lun now at an end, the heroes could return home. But tragedy soon struck. When Danny tried to heal a young child named Bobby Wright he was killed by the child's powerful alter ego, who went by the name of Captain Hero. Luke Cage was seen standing over Iron Fist's body and blamed for the death. Iron Fist was apparently dead and Cage was once again a hunted man. But all was not as it seemed...

POWER MAN & IRON FIST #120 (NOV. 1985) Iron Fist unleashed his full fury on Chiantang but it was only when Lei-Kung used the mystical sword Dragonslayer to open a portal that the creature was finally defeated.

NAMOR THE SUB-MARINER #16 (JUL. 1991) Namor was confused by Iron Fist's rants about the Fantastic Four as they fought. It was only later Namor realized he was facing the Super-Skrull.

The Power of Chi

Iron Fist wasn't dead... but he wasn't exactly alive either. He was trapped in a H'ylthri pod outside K'un-Lun, his chi energy feeding the city's ancient enemies.

At one point it seemed Danny had returned from the dead. He "appeared" in the Savage Land alongside Ward Meachum (Harold Meachum's brother). Even Misty Knight was fooled by the impostor. Namor the Sub-Mariner was opposing an ecological disaster that Rand-Meachum Inc. was planning in the Savage Land when he came into conflict with this Iron Fist—only to learn it was actually the shape-changing Super-Skrull.

Misty and the Prince of Atlantis soon uncovered the truth: during Danny's last trip to K'un-Lun, he had been replaced by a member of the H'ylthri and the real Danny was trapped in a pod. Doctor Strange helped Misty, Colleen Wing, and Namor travel to K'un-Lun, where they found the city destroyed by the H'ylthri and its population held in pods to feed their young. When an unconscious Danny heard Misty call for help, he regained his senses and punched his way out, going on to help defeat the H'ylthri and free K'un-Lun's citizens.

Once back home, Danny learned that the Super-Skrull who had impersonated him had also pretended to be the young hero Bobby Wright, and had been placed there by Master Khan to kill Iron Fist. When the sorcerer learned that Danny was still alive, he appeared and stole Namor's memory in revenge for his interference. Iron Fist helped Namor restore his memory, and the Prince of Atlantis seemingly killed Khan.

Danny was soon back in action as Iron Fist, helping Spider-Man take on the symbiote Carnage's forces and fighting a reborn Steel Serpent. He also learned his half-sister, Miranda, was still alive after—under H'ylthri orders—she tried to steal an artifact known as the Zodiac Key.

NAMOR THE SUB-MARINER #22 (JAN. 1992) When the real Iron Fist heard Namor and his friends fighting the H'ylthri, he focused the last of his chi to escape the pod he was trapped in.

When it seemed the Avengers and Fantastic Four had died fighting the mutant menace known as Onslaught, Danny formed a new incarnation of Heroes for Hire—in the belief it would bring back hope to the world. Once again he teamed up with Luke Cage, alongside heroes such as Ant-Man, the Black Knight, and a new incarnation of White Tiger. During his time on the team, Danny revealed to Misty Knight that he had found a cauldron belonging to his father that connected his heart with K'un-Lun and gave him the power to make the city materialize in their world. Heroes for Hire eventually disbanded after Tony Stark's company bought out Rand-Meachum.

Shortly after, Japanese teenage martial arts prodigy Junzo Muto stole the power of Shou-Lao from Danny using an ancient rite. The teenager kidnapped Misty Knight, attempting to lure Danny to Tokyo where he could make K'un-Lun appear.

Muto was head of a splintered branch of the ninja clan known as the Hand, and planned to use K'un-Lun as a base to conquer the world and bring the infamous assassins out of the shadows. Iron Fist was joined by a number of allies, including Wolverine, in an attempt to stop him. As K'un-Lun started to materialize over Tokyo, Danny freed Yu-Ti, the city's ruler, from captivity. Ku'n-Lun's Dragon-Kings had been trapped in

IRON FIST WOLVERINE #4 (FEB. 2001) While fighting Junzo Muto and the Hand, Wolverine and Iron Fist also found themselves facing K'un-Lun's Dragon-Kings.

BLACK PANTHER #38 (JAN. 2002) A disguised Chiantang restored Iron Fist's power but moved his chi out of balance and imposed a hypnotic command that forced him to fight the Black Panther.

their dragon forms and forced to align with Muto. With the transference of K'un-Lun nearly final, Yu-Ti stabbed Danny, realizing that only by killing Danny could his link with K'un-Lun be severed. Iron Fist's spirit left his body and was about to pass to Feng-Tu—K'un-Lun's land of the dead—when the spirits of Danny's parents told him he could remain on Earth if he wanted to—the magic from K'un-Lun's appearance giving him the ability to do so. Muto escaped, and Danny found himself with some confused dragons to look after.

Shortly after, Danny was dragged into an attempt by Nightshade (an old enemy of Luke Cage) to gain revenge on the Wakandan leader Black Panther. Nightshade brought the Dragon-Lord Chiantang back to life and the Black Dragon (as Nightshade preferred to call Chiantang) gave Iron Fist back his powers—while also planting controls in his mind that made him attack Black Panther. Nightshade had not managed to bring Chiantang back to life successfully, however, and flaws in his new DNA were going to doom him until Black Panther tried a new tactic: rather than fighting Chiantang, he used science to save his life. Chiantang relented in his attack, knowing that he now owed Black Panther. For his part, Danny had regained the power of Shou-Lao, and could again truly call himself Iron Fist.

Outlaw Heroes

Following his return from the dead, Danny reclaimed control of the Rand Corporation after the collapse of Stark-Fujikawa. He also took on the role of Daredevil while Matt Murdock was in prison—even mimicking his friend's unique martial arts moves.

While acting as Daredevil, Danny found himself caught up in the superhuman civil war—when Tony Stark tried to force his fellow Super Heroes to give up their secret identities for a government register—fighting on the side of Captain America's anti-registration forces. Following the war, Danny started to learn more about the history of Iron Fist. Later, he was one of the heroes tested by the Hand's ninja assassins to see if he would be worthy of becoming their new leader, a role they eventually offered to Daredevil.

Iron Fist continued to fight alongside the "Secret Avengers" Captain America had formed during the civil war, only this time, with Cap supposedly dead, working under the leadership of Luke Cage. In-between all the danger, there were moments of peace: most notably when Luke and Jessica Jones revealed that their baby girl would be called Danielle—named after Cage's closest friend.

"War changes everything."

IRON FIST

Through all this, Danny's lawyer, Jeryn Hogarth, skillfully protected him from the new anti-Super Hero laws.

When Danny realized Daredevil's old ally Maya Lopez was in trouble—or possibly dead—he turned to his teammates for help. They had been hiding out in Doctor Strange's Sanctum Sanctorum and traveled to Japan to rescue—or avenge—Maya. They became involved in a huge confrontation with the Hand—now led by the fearsome martial artist, Elektra. They discovered Maya had been killed and resurrected as a Hand assassin, but Iron Fist and Doctor Strange worked together to help Maya overcome the programming. She then killed Elektra—only for Elektra to be revealed as a shape-shifting Skrull. It was the first clue that the Skrulls had infiltrated Earth's heroes and Danny remained with the Avengers as they fought against the aliens' secret invasion of Earth.

Danny was also on the front line during Norman Osborn's Dark Reign, when the ex-villain became the new director of H.A.M.M.E.R. (S.H.I.E.L.D.'s replacement agency). He briefly left the Avengers, but helped them out when Osborn captured Luke Cage.

Opposite page: CIVIL WAR: CHOOSING SIDES #1 (DEC. 2006) Danny took on the role of Daredevil, even changing his own fighting style to match the Man Without Fear's. Only their closest friends could spot the difference.

NEW AVENGERS #29 (JUN. 2007) Iron Fist joined Spider-Woman, Doctor Strange, Luke Cage, Wolverine, and Spider-Man in a "Secret Avengers" team following the superhuman civil war.

In the aftermath of Osborn's fall from grace, Danny remained an Avenger and joined a new roster led by Luke Cage—who was placed there by Steve Rogers. Danny even lent Cage a dollar so he could "buy" Avengers mansion from Tony Stark and use it as a base for the new team. Iron Fist was soon at the center of the action as the team fought against supernatural demons seeking the magical talisman the Eye of Agamotto. The adventure saw Danny gain a new outfit as he became possessed and pulled to the demons' dimension. Eventually, the heroes ended the threat and Danny was recovered.

NEW AVENGERS #4 (NOV. 2010)
Danny's spiritual training helped keep him alive when he traveled to a magical dimension with the Eye of Agamotto.

AVENGERS VS. X-MEN #10 (OCT. 2012) Iron Fist tried to protect Hope from the Phoenix-possessed Cyclops, although the teenager and Scarlet Witch were later to prove more than a match for the X-Man.

AVENGERS VS. X-MEN #6 (AUG. 2010) The power of the Iron Fist and the Phoenix Force have been connected for millennia, as written in some of K'un-Lun's most sacred texts.

Danny's life in K'un-Lun and new knowledge of the history of the Iron Fist helped inform the New Avengers when the destructive Phoenix Force returned to Earth. Conflict broke out with the X-Men over what to do with the mutant named Hope Summers—the Phoenix's intended host. After several violent confrontations between the teams, Iron Fist took Hope and the New Avengers to K'un-Lun, after learning that Fongji Wu—a previous Iron Fist—had become a host for the Phoenix centuries before. Her role as that era's Iron Fist enabled her to contain and control the deadly force and Danny believed Hope could do the same.

Though Danny thought he would be the one to train Hope, Yu-Ti used a scrying pool and found it was Spider-Man who would teach her. As Hope trained, Iron Fist fought alongside the team against the X-Men, until only Cyclops remained, now wielding the full power of the Phoenix. Hope joined forces with the Scarlet Witch to defeat Cyclops, driving the entity from him and becoming Phoenix herself. She then manipulated the power to undo the damage it had caused.

Iron Fist helped the Avengers against Norman Osborn's dark version of the team and Daniel Drumm's attempt to destroy them in revenge for the seeming death of his brother, Doctor Voodoo. The team eventually disbanded, and Danny once again went his own way.

NEW AVENGERS #23 (MAY 2012) When Iron Fist fought Osborn's Dark Avengers, he found himself fighting Gorgon. He defeated him with the help of Daredevil.

IMMORTAL IRON FIST #5 (JUN. 2007)
Danny fought Hydra alongside Orson Randall, the previous Iron Fist. Orson could channel his chi through his bullets, adapting his fighting style into "gun fu."

Immortal Weapons

Danny Rand's understanding of his role as Iron Fist went through major changes when he met Orson Randall, who had been Iron Fist since the early 20th century.

Danny's company was under threat from Wai-Go, a Chinese corporation. Led by Mr. Xao, it was secretly a front for the terrorist organization Hydra and was seeking to destroy K'un-Lun. Xao himself was actually one of the immortal lightning lords—Randall had killed his two brothers and Xao wanted revenge. Davos, the Steel Serpent, also allied himself with Xao. Randall gave Danny the *Book of the Iron Fist*,

a sacred tome that recorded the lives of all 66 previous Iron Fists. Danny learned that his father had been Orson's ward (and sometime sidekick) before he left for K'un-Lun. When Davos and his forces attacked the two Iron Fists, Orson was killed, but he passed on his chi to Danny, increasing his power. The Steel Serpent fled when he realized he was no match for Danny's boosted abilities. Before the dust had settled, Lei-Kung and Yu-Ti arrived to take Danny home to K'un-Lun. It was time for the Tournament of the Heavenly Cities.

> "This is the fight I was born for."
>
> **IRON FIST**

There were six other Heavenly Cities and every 88 years their celestial paths converged, allowing parts of each to join together, forming an area called the Heart of Heaven. Each city put forward its own champion, known as an Immortal Weapon, and the winning city gained the ability to connect to Earth every decade—the losing cities would be cut off for increasing periods depending on how well their champion performed. Iron Fist would be K'un-Lun's Immortal Weapon, while Steel Serpent represented the Crane Mother, ruler of the city of K'un-Zi. The other champions were Fat Cobra, Bride of Nine Spiders, Dog Brother #1, Tiger's Beautiful Daughter, and the Prince of Orphans.

The night before Danny was due to fight Fat Cobra, the daughter of Orson Randall visited Danny. She was working with Lei-Kung to bring revolution to K'un-Lun and overthrow its corrupt ruler, Yu-Ti. To this end, Lei-Kung had trained a secret army of female warriors called the Army of Thunder. Danny used a hidden gateway created long before by Orson's father to briefly return to Earth and learn more about his predecessor.

On his return, Danny realized Xao's plan was to send a train filled with explosives through a portal to destroy K'un-Lun, and shared this knowledge with the Prince of Orphans. They convinced the other Immortal Weapons to join their fight. As Xao opened the portal to K'un-Lun, he found himself facing all the Immortal Weapons. They were more than a match for Xao's forces—especially with help from Luke Cage, Colleen Wing, and Misty Knight. Defeated, Xao threw himself to his death after revealing that there was an Eighth City. Yu-Ti escaped when he saw the Army of Thunder, and Lei-Kung became K'un-Lun's new ruler. Orson's daughter took the name Sparrow and became the new Thunderer.

Above: IMMORTAL IRON FIST #8 (OCT. 2007) The other Immortal Weapons: Fat Cobra (Peng Lai Island); The Bride of Nine Spiders (Kingdom of Spiders); Dog Brother #1 (Under City); Tiger's Beautiful Daughter (Tiger Island); Prince of Orphans (Z'Gambo); Steel Serpent (K'un-Zi).

Left: IMMORTAL IRON FIST #14 (JUN. 2008) The Immortal Weapons joined forces with Iron Fist to prevent Hydra destroying K'un-Lun, realizing that if Hydra succeeded, their own cities would also be destroyed.

Inset left: IMMORTAL IRON FIST #13 (MAY 2008) When Xao opened his gate to K'un-Lun, Iron Fist and the Immortal Weapons were waiting for him.

Having returned to Earth with the Immortal Weapons, Danny opened the Thunder Dojo in Harlem, New York City. He also defeated Zhou Cheng, a servant of the demon Ch'i-Lin, who fed off the energy of Iron Fists, killing many of them when they turned 33. Danny went back to K'un-Lun when its new ruler, Lei-Kung, asked him to free innocent people trapped in the hellish Eighth City. The city had been established to house all the monsters, demons, and criminals that had once threatened the Heavenly Cities; but K'un-Lun's previous ruler had also sent his political enemies there. Only Immortal Weapons could open the gates to the Eighth City. Once inside, Danny and his fellow warriors were captured and thrown into a brutal arena. The city's ruler turned out to be one of the first Iron Fists, Quan Yaozu, who had sacrificed himself to make sure the demons didn't escape the city. He felt betrayed by K'un-Lun when its people had ignored his sacrifice, and planned to use the Immortal Weapons to escape the city and destroy K'un-Lun. When events took a twist and Iron Fist saved his life, Quan Yaozu realized K'un-Lun might not be the corrupt place it once was, and sought a more peaceful resolution.

Soon after, K'un-Lun was destroyed by the One—a demonic entity that combined Danny's father with the power of the android that Danny had fought long ago for the right to take on the dragon Shou-Lao. The One beheaded Lei-Kung, while Davos once again betrayed K'un-Lun and attacked Sparrow, blinding her. A young monk named Pei escaped with the last egg of Shou-Lao and turned to Danny for help. Danny was no match for the One at first and was badly beaten. With the help of Sparrow, Pei—who had become a new Iron Fist—and a robotics genius monk named Fooh, Danny gained energy from the One and defeated him, though Davos killed Shou-Lao. As K'un-Lun's survivors returned home to rebuild their lives, Sparrow left Pei with Danny to train. Pei had one last surprise. She had brought K'un-Lun's dragons back to life. Danny had a new pet: Shou-Lao.

Danny later felt himself cut off from the power of the Iron Fist and traveled the world trying to regain his chi. Eventually, a martial artist named Choshin invited him to a tournament on the island of Liu-Shi. The islanders had left K'un-Lun a century before and set up their own sanctuary. It was a trap. The seven masters, styled after different animals, planned to steal Iron Fist's power, while Choshin wanted Liu-Shi to replace K'un-Lun as one of the Heavenly Cities. When Danny realized he was fighting for the future of K'un-Lun, his power returned and he defeated Choshin. With K'un-Lun in danger, Danny needed to find a way home.

After a brief run-in with a possessed Shang-Chi, Danny teamed up with a reformed Sabretooth to save K'un-Lun from Choshin and his legions. Choshin used the stolen *Book of the Iron Fist* to open a portal to K'un-Lun. As Choshin's army invaded, all seemed lost—especially when Danny vanished with the tome. Just as Choshin's forces seemed victorious, Danny returned riding Shou-Lao. The pair soon turned the tide of battle and encouraged the inhabitants of K'un-Lun to rise up against the invaders. After a vicious fight with Danny, Choshin tried to flee—only to be eaten by a hungry Shou-Lao. K'un-Lun was saved and a new era was beginning—with Danny Rand the Iron Fist once again its Immortal Weapon.

Left and inset: IRON FIST #77 (APR. 2018)
Lei-Kung's daughter, Sparrow, led K'un-Lun's forces against Choshin's army, as Iron Fist returned on Shou-Lao to turn the tide of battle against the invaders.

Defending the Innocent

As Daredevil Matt Murdock took over the ninja cult known as the Hand and was slowly corrupted, Danny Rand and Luke Cage met teen hero-for-hire Victor Alvarez.

The son of one of Danny and Luke's old enemies, Victor had been the sole survivor of a building blown up by the assassin Bullseye and only survived by taking in the chi of those around him. Iron Fist and Cage tried to help him, but an angry Alvarez managed to drain Danny's Iron Fist chi and use it against him. Impressed by the teen—who had briefly been a student at Danny's Thunder Dojo—Danny began to train Victor in martial arts and taught him how to control his chi-power. Alvarez became the new Power Man and joined the heroes in their fight against the Hand.

Meanwhile, Danny remained in contact with the Immortal Weapons—champions from the six other Heavenly Cities. He fought alongside them when the followers of Cul—the ancient Norse God of Fear—tried to open the gates of the Eighth City. One of Cul's followers, Nul, Breaker of Worlds, remained free after Cul's defeat. The Hulk turned to his old allies in the Defenders for help in stopping Nul. Iron Fist joined them—mainly because they needed someone with a private jet. Danny was puzzled that the Defenders couldn't remember their earlier adventures together. When they located an ancient machine called the Concordance Engine, Danny realized their amnesia was due to a mystical force. The Concordance Engine—one of several—guarded by Prester John, was created to protect the world from suicidal cosmic beings called Death Celestials. It had the power to prevent people acknowledging

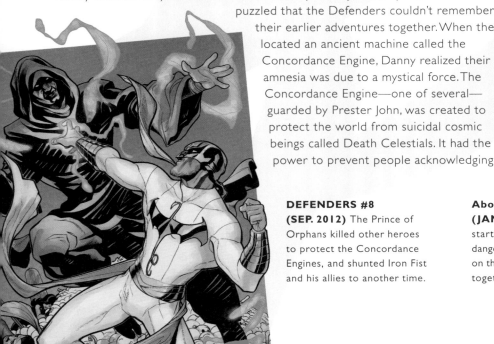

DEFENDERS #8 (SEP. 2012) The Prince of Orphans killed other heroes to protect the Concordance Engines, and shunted Iron Fist and his allies to another time.

Above: DEFENDERS #7 (JAN. 2018) When Diamondback started selling a variation of the dangerous Mutant Growth Hormone on the streets, the Defenders came together to stop him.

Right: DEFENDERS #4 (OCT. 2017) Despite Diamondback severely injuring him, Iron Fist used his chi to rise again and defeat the villain—before confiding in teammate Jessica Jones that he was in excruciating pain from Diamondback's attack.

its existence for its own protection. The situation brought Danny into conflict with the Prince of Orphans, who had been killing the other Immortal Weapons in an attempt to protect the Concordance Engines.

As the Defenders confronted him, the Prince of Orphans shunted them to a parallel Earth. When Danny and his allies found their way home, it was to an Earth devastated by a Death Celestial. Realizing the Concordance Engines must remain undiscovered to maintain their reality, Doctor Strange astrally projected back in time to make sure he was elsewhere when the Hulk came asking for his help—making sure this incarnation of the Defenders was never formed, the Immortal Weapons were not killed, and Earth was never destroyed.

Danny's involvement in the next incarnation of the Defenders was far more street-level. Danny, Luke Cage, Jessica Jones, and Daredevil joined forces when Hydra took over the US, defending Manhattan from the crime-cult's forces. Following Hydra's defeat, they stayed together, only to be attacked by Cage's former friend turned enemy Diamondback when he made a play to become the new Kingpin of Crime. The four heroes soon found themselves in the center of a gang war as Black Cat and the Hood also made moves to take over local crime operations. In a fight with Danny, Diamondback—his strength enhanced by a new version of the Mutant Growth Hormone—seemed to break Danny's back, only for Danny to rise to his feet and leave Diamondback badly beaten.

DEFENDERS #7 (JAN. 2018)
Elektra and Danny were evenly matched, their fight crashing through several buildings until the power of the Iron Fists gave Danny the edge.

Ninja assassin Elektra was also tracking potential new Kingpins, which saw her fight Iron Fist for the first time after she broke into his office—both were impressed with the other's combat skills. No sooner had the Defenders ended Diamondback's attempt to be Kingpin than the Hood, powered by stolen Norn Stones, made his move. Danny called on a few old friends to take down the criminal and his allies.

The Defenders split, but Danny and Luke once again opened up shop as Heroes for Hire. The duo soon found themselves bringing old enemy Black Mariah to justice. They also came into conflict with Alex Wilder, a onetime hero who had turned to crime and was trying to create a new incarnation of the Pryde—the criminal cartel his parents were once part of. Danny ended up in Ryker's Island Penitentiary as a result of a computer program Wilder had devised which could create criminal files on innocent people. Danny and Luke eventually took down the villain, but were soon called back into action by the Avengers to help fight against Malekith the Dark Elf's invasion of Earth.

While Danny and Luke often find themselves caught up in their own personal dramas, each is there for the other. They will always be firm friends, defenders of the innocent and, when needed, heroes for hire.

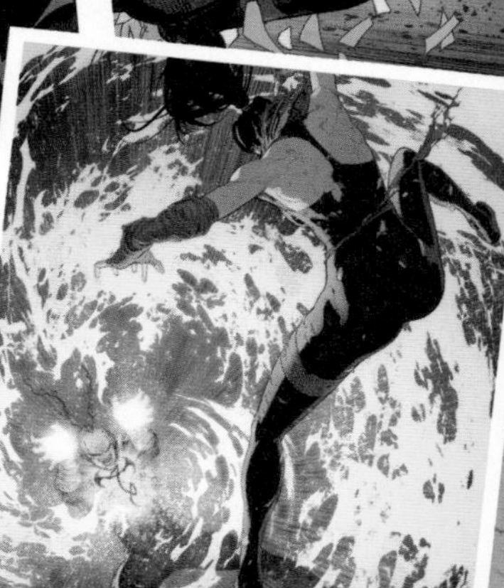

"It is a dangerous thing, to believe oneself the master of a fighting art."

IRON FIST

DRAGONS AND TIGERS

STREET-LEVEL HEROES

The Daughters of the Dragon, Sons of the Tiger, and White Tiger are all martial artists of amazing skill and ability. From the deadly samurai tradition of Colleen Wing through to the mystically powered martial arts of the most recent White Tiger, Ava Ayala, these are heroes who have risked all to save others.

Colleen and her partner Misty Knight have proven to be two of the toughest private investigators in the business. Known as the Daughters of the Dragon, they are more than able to hold their own alongside their friends Luke Cage and Danny Rand. They have faced off against the likes of villains Sabretooth and the Constrictor and lived to tell the tale. Colleen has even passed her skills on to Misty, augmenting Misty's own fighting style and making her even more dangerous—especially with her powerful cybernetic arm. The Sons of the Tiger, even without their mystical Amulets of Power, have extraordinary mixed martial arts skills—originally taught to them by their teacher, Master Kee. Their skills were transferred through the talisman to the first White Tiger, Hector Ayala. While Hector's time as a hero ended in tragedy, his heroic nature proved to be an inspiration for others—especially his niece Angela Del Toro and his younger sister Ava Ayala—both of whom have served as the White Tiger. Even before becoming heroes, the two had spent a lifetime practicing martial arts and the mystical talisman they wore served only to increase the skill they already had.

While all these street-level heroes come from very different backgrounds, there is one thing that they have in common: deadly hands of kung fu!

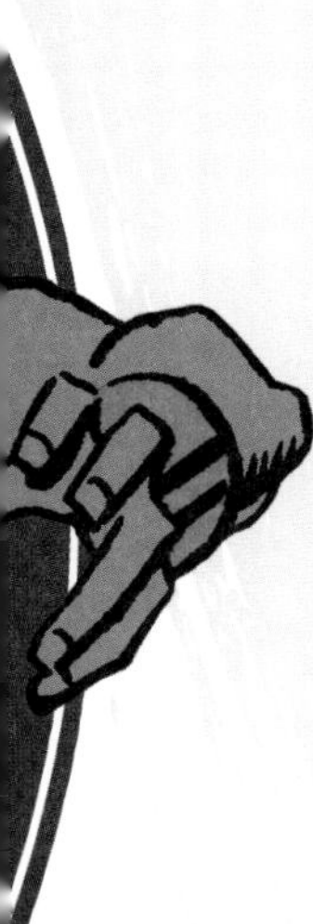

Opposite top: DAUGHTERS OF THE DRAGON #5 (JUL. 2006) When samurai-turned-detective Colleen Wing teamed up with ex-cop Misty Knight they soon gained the name "Daughters of the Dragon" due to their ferocious fighting skills.

Left: MARVEL TEAM-UP #40 (DEC. 1975) After three friends with a love of kung fu inherited mystical Tiger amulets, they found that their strength, speed, and fighting skills increased. They became the Sons of the Tiger.

Colleen Wing: Samurai Detective

Colleen Wing is one of the deadliest women alive. Her father, Lee Wing, was an American historian specializing in Asian history, while her Japanese mother was descended from a long line of samurai and daimyo.

Following her mother's death, Colleen was raised in Japan by her grandfather, Kenji Ozawa. Kenji had worked for the Japanese secret service and, like his brother Osama, had no male heirs left alive to pass his skills on to. Both trained Colleen in the ways of the samurai—the ancient code of Bushido ("the way of the warrior"). It was a harsh regime. Each day started with a ten-mile run in the mountains, often barefoot. She was taught kendo from the age of 12 and given a Meito katana—a legendary sword of unrivaled quality—knowing that she should only ever unsheathe it when she wished to draw blood. While she mastered the Japanese martial arts, her training and upbringing made her prefer a solitary, stoic life. Many referred to her as "the woman who never laughed."

DAUGHTERS OF THE DRAGON #6 (AUG. 2006) Colleen and Misty gained their nickname during a fight with the Steel Serpent. He had intended it to be an insult, but the name stuck.

"Part of me is a samurai… and that part kills!"

COLLEEN WING

That all changed when she met Mercedes "Misty" Knight. Colleen had moved to New York to be near her father, when she was caught up in a firefight in Manhattan's West Side. She was saved by Misty—a police officer in the NYPD's bomb squad—and the two quickly became firm friends. Misty helped bring Colleen out of herself, and when Misty was caught in a terrorist explosion and lost an arm, it was Colleen who helped her recover and deal with the trauma.

Colleen started to train her new friend in martial arts—which Misty combined with her own street style to create what she sometimes referred to as "Harlem kung fu." The two friends opened up their own detective agency, Knightwing Restorations, and started to gain a reputation. Their fearsome fighting skills meant they also gained a new nickname: Daughters of the Dragon.

TOTALLY AWESOME HULK #11 (DEFENDERS VARIANT COVER) (DEC. 2016) Colleen gained many of Danny Rand's kung fu skills after sharing his chi. The two often train together.

Above: IRON FIST #7 (SEP. 1976)
Colleen tore through Angar's men with a tsuki strike, parrying an overhand naginata attack, before launching a migi-do (chest) assault to bring her face to face with Angar.

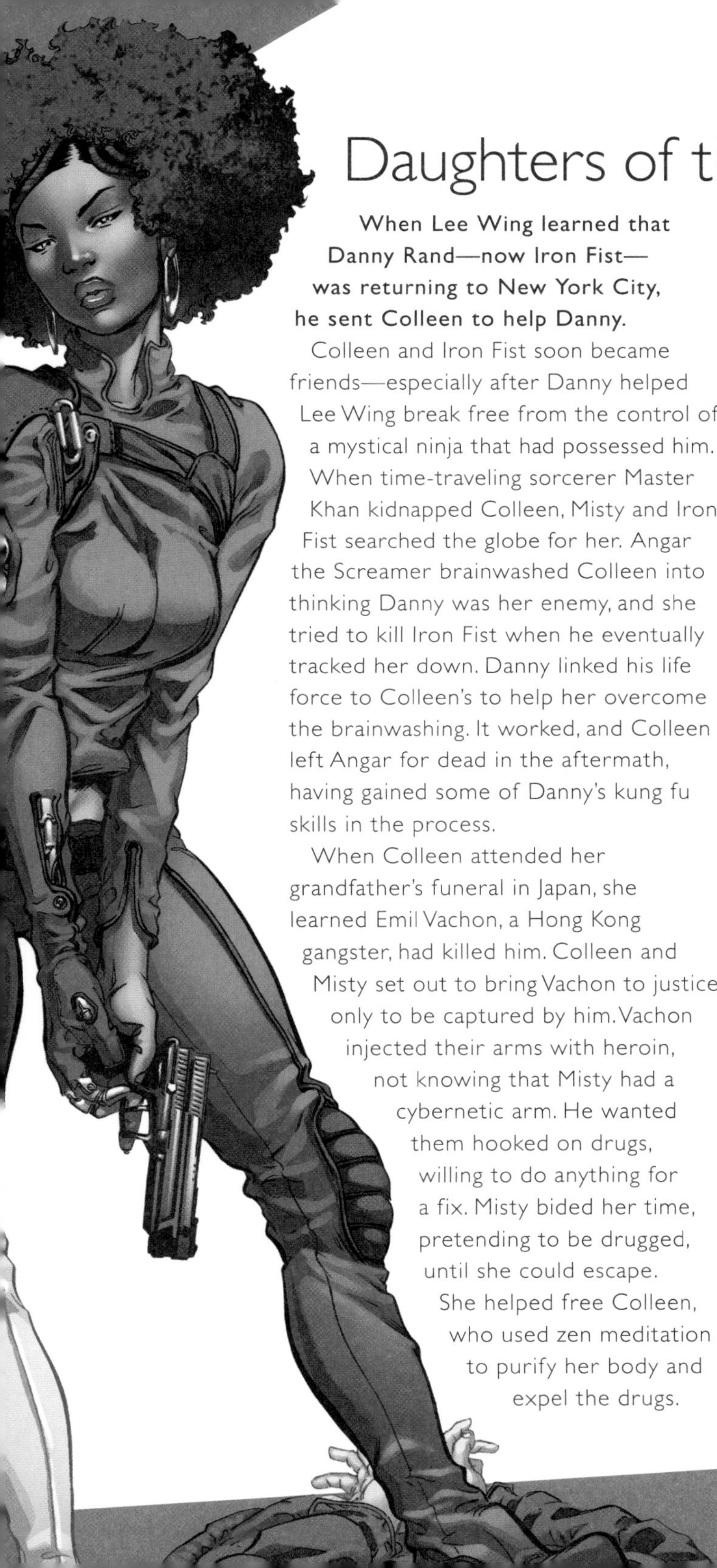

Daughters of the Dragon

When Lee Wing learned that Danny Rand—now Iron Fist—was returning to New York City, he sent Colleen to help Danny.

Colleen and Iron Fist soon became friends—especially after Danny helped Lee Wing break free from the control of a mystical ninja that had possessed him. When time-traveling sorcerer Master Khan kidnapped Colleen, Misty and Iron Fist searched the globe for her. Angar the Screamer brainwashed Colleen into thinking Danny was her enemy, and she tried to kill Iron Fist when he eventually tracked her down. Danny linked his life force to Colleen's to help her overcome the brainwashing. It worked, and Colleen left Angar for dead in the aftermath, having gained some of Danny's kung fu skills in the process.

When Colleen attended her grandfather's funeral in Japan, she learned Emil Vachon, a Hong Kong gangster, had killed him. Colleen and Misty set out to bring Vachon to justice only to be captured by him. Vachon injected their arms with heroin, not knowing that Misty had a cybernetic arm. He wanted them hooked on drugs, willing to do anything for a fix. Misty bided her time, pretending to be drugged, until she could escape. She helped free Colleen, who used zen meditation to purify her body and expel the drugs. Still suffering the after-effects, Colleen sought out Vachon and killed him.

Misty and Colleen helped the X-Men take down infamous arms dealer Moses Magnum. Colleen was attracted to the mutant Cyclops, but their relationship was short-lived. By then, Misty was in a relationship with Danny Rand and Daughters of the Dragon often worked with Danny and Luke Cage. Through Danny, Colleen met Bob Diamond, actor and martial artist. For short time, Colleen and Bob became a couple but their relationship wasn't the luckiest. They were shot by snipers, attacked by a ninja, electrocuted by the assassin Constrictor, and turned to glass by Chemistro, before eventually parting.

Colleen's friendship with Misty became strained when her friend started to date cop Tyrone King (who later turned out to be Khan in disguise) behind Danny's back. This led to Colleen journeying to K'un-Lun without her partner when Danny faced the dragon Chiantang. Misty and Colleen together uncovered the truth about Danny's "death" when Misty saw the Super-Skrull impersonating him. After Namor defeated the Super-Skrull, Misty and Colleen learned the Danny they had buried had been a H'ylthri imposter. They returned to K'un-Lun with Namor and freed the real Danny from the H'ylthri.

Left: DAUGHTERS OF THE DRAGON #1 (MAR. 2006) After Colleen and Misty became bail bondswomen they successfully apprehended super-powered villains such as Rhino and Orka.

"Girl, there's about to be all kinds of kung fu up in here!"

MISTY KNIGHT

Knightwing Restorations later became bail bond agents, taking on mid-level superhumans, mutants, and mad scientists as clients. When they tried to bring in petty crook Freezer Burn, they became entangled in mob queen Celia Ricadonna's attempt to auction off a microchip created by the Mad Thinker. One of Freezer Burn's partners, Humbug, turned to Misty for protection, and gave her the chip, which he had unwittingly stolen from Ricadonna. Misty used her cybernetic arm to read it and learned it could be used to destabilize the world economy. Ricadonna confronted Misty and retrieved the chip by slicing off Misty's cybernetic arm. Colleen called in a favor from Tony Stark to get Misty a new, improved arm—one laced with diamonds and Vibranium. Misty and Colleen then infiltrated the auction Ricadonna was hosting and, with a little help from Iron Fist, reclaimed the chip—with Misty getting her revenge on Ricadonna.

The duo went on to create a new incarnation of Heroes for Hire during the superhuman civil war. While they tried to remain neutral during the war, they agreed to track down criminals for S.H.I.E.L.D.

Right: DAUGHTERS OF THE DRAGON #5 (JUL. 2006) Before crashing Ricadonna's auction, Misty and Colleen turned to the Punisher for help with their armory. Iron Fist then joined them for the assault.

The team split when Misty handed over Savage Land native Moon-Boy to the authorities, despite Colleen's objections. Misty, under the influence of the criminal mastermind Puppet Master, then started a new Heroes for Hire operation, but it was short-lived.

When Daredevil became leader of the Hand, he lured Colleen to his side by revealing her mother had once led an all-female Hand cadre of ninjas called the Nail. Colleen led a new incarnation of the Nail and tried to use it as a force for good—stopping human traffickers and slavers. She soon realized Daredevil's methods were going too far and joined with Iron Fist and other heroes to bring down Matt Murdock's Shadowland.

Misty went on to fight alongside the Fearless Defenders when the Asgardian Valkyrie formed a new team. She became an FBI agent, while Colleen remained a free spirit. The pair teamed up to track down some missing teens—with Misty rescuing Colleen when she was captured by Bunraku, an aging criminal who was draining blood from the teens to stay alive.

S.H.I.E.L.D. agent Nick Fury, Jr. later hired Colleen and Misty to track down Rutherford Winner—an agent created by Hydra to be the ultimate killer. When they realized Winner had been exploited by S.H.I.E.L.D., they ensured he got the help he needed. In return, when Emila Vachon, daughter of Hong Kong crimelord Emil, captured and brainwashed Colleen and Misty, Winner helped them break free. Colleen defeated Vachon but let her live, hoping to end the cycle of violence. Misty and Colleen's friendship was stronger than ever and the Daughters of the Dragon were back in action.

DAUGHTERS OF THE DRAGON #1 (JAN. 2019) While investigating missing teenagers, Colleen Wing found herself attacked by killer Japanese puppets.

DAUGHTERS OF THE DRAGON #3 (MAR. 2019) Colleen refused to kill Emila Vachon, though she did sever Vachon's hand during their final confrontation.

Sons of the Tiger

When assassins killed Master Kee, owner of the Tiger Dojo in New York, his adopted son Lin Sun and Lin's closest friends swore to avenge his death.

They were helped by three mystical pendants that Master Kee gave Lin as he died—amulets that bestowed amazing abilities on the trio. The first was the head of a tiger—the school's symbol—and the other two its claws. When the friends used them and recited a special inscription, they found their strength and speed had tripled and they could share each other's martial arts skills.

Master Kee was the closest thing Lin had to a father. Kee had rescued Lin when he was just a baby and his parents had been killed by revolutionaries. Abe Brown was from a rough part of New York and took up martial arts after being attacked by racists. Robert (Bob) Diamond was a rich and successful actor who practiced martial arts in an attempt to star in action films.

All three had little in common, but their love of kung fu soon made them firm friends. What they didn't realize was that the amulets that gave them their power were part of an ancient statue called the Jade Tiger, an idol once owned by sorcerer Master Khan who had been a god to the people of the legendary city of K'un-Lun. Going by the name the Sons of the Tiger, the trio soon uncovered a conspiracy behind their teacher's death.

Agents working for a group called the Silent Ones attacked them. While trying to find out more about their attackers, the Tigers rescued martial artist Lotus Shinchuko from the villains' control. Bob was attracted to her, but didn't realize the Silent Ones were still able to control Lotus using a device planted in the back of her neck. She turned on her new friends and nearly killed Bob and Abe. Lin removed the device and soon discovered they could use it to locate the Silent Ones.

They found themselves on another plane of existence, taken there by the Silent Ones, and learned their enemies were the survivors of an ancient godlike race. Their leader had been testing the trio to see if their bodies would be strong enough to act as new vessels for his race. He raised the dormant Silent Ones, the Sons of the Tiger finding themselves fighting a legion of zombie-like beings. After a fight, Lin kicked the Silent Ones' leader through an inter-dimensional gateway, ending the threat.

DEADLY HANDS OF KUNG FU #16 (SEP. 1975)
While investigating a corrupt prison warden, the Sons of the Tiger found themselves fighting killer prison guards and the National Guard.

"When three are called and stand as one, as one they'll fight, their will be done… for each is born anew the Tiger's Son."

LIN SUN

With their quest for vengeance at an end, the Sons of the Tiger opened up a new martial arts school in an old warehouse on the lower east side of Manhattan. While training one day, they investigated a noise coming from the neighboring warehouse, only to find the villain Crime-Master auctioning off an unconscious Johnny Storm and Spider-Man. They helped free the two Super Heroes and defeat Crime-Master and his allies.

Tensions arose in the team when Lin and Lotus started having feelings for each other. Before long, there was a full-blown love triangle, with Lotus eventually leaving Bob for Lin. The jilted actor then turned on his friends, striking Abe, who quit the team. Then Bob and Lin came to blows. Lin realized the Sons of the Tiger were no more, and tossed away the amulets.

Above: MARVEL TEAM-UP #40 (DEC. 1975) The Sons of the Tiger rescued Spider-Man and the Human Torch, but were then caught up in a fight between the Big Man and Crime-Master.

Right: DEADLY HANDS OF KUNG FU #19 (DEC. 1975) While Bob and Lin had a ferocious fight, leaving both men cut and bruised, they parted as friends, albeit no longer Sons of the Tiger.

Years later, the three friends reconciled, opening a new kung fu school in San Francisco's Chinatown. It was here that they joined Wolverine in an effort to fight local gangs.

When Lin originally discarded the amulets they were picked up by a young man, Hector Ayala, who transformed into the White Tiger. Hector was from the South Bronx. His father worked three jobs to keep the family afloat and deal with the fallout from Hector's brother, Filippo, who had a drug problem. At first, Hector couldn't even remember being White Tiger. After fighting as the hero, he would regain his senses out of costume, sweating and trembling like an addict. It was only when Hector saw images of his alter ego in a newspaper with the same amulets he possessed that he realized the truth. Hector would not have an easy time as a hero—and it was a role that would end in tragedy.

Left: DEADLY HANDS OF KUNG FU #22 (MAR. 1976) Hector only learned that he was the White Tiger when he saw a photo of his costumed alter ego in the *Daily Globe*.

Right and below: SPECTACULAR SPIDER-MAN #9 (AUG. 1977) When Hector became the White Tiger he gained the martial arts skills of others who had used the amulets—such as the Sons of the Tiger.

Hector Ayala took time to come to terms with his dual role. After run-ins with criminal the Prowler and a vengeful Jack of Hearts, Hector asked his brother Filippo to help him locate the cartel that had been feeding him drugs.

Only Hector had already worked out the track marks on his brother's arm were fake. Filippo wasn't an addict, but a dealer. He was part of a criminal organization called the Corporation. White Tiger was joined by new allies Iron Fist, Shang-Chi, Jack of Hearts, and ex-cop Blackbyrd to bring down the cartel. Defeated, Filippo knew he had failed, and he blew himself up.

Soon after, White Tiger saved the life of Sons of the Tiger member Bob Diamond and began to learn the history of the amulets. The trio offered him a place on their team, but Hector wanted to forge his own path, joining Empire State University. However, he soon had a run-in with Spider-Man after the web-slinger believed that the White Tiger had stolen a precious manuscript. In fact, a college lecturer had taken it while disguised as the hero. The confusion led to the White Tiger and Spider-Man facing off, until Hector rescued some bystanders, convincing Spidey he was fighting for good.

Shortly after the episode, the White Tiger's identity was revealed to the public. This led to tragedy, when disaffected army veteran Gideon Mace attacked and killed most of Hector's close family, with only his youngest sister, Ava, surviving. Hector himself was shot and nearly killed after tracking down Mace. Spider-Man eventually brought Mace to justice, but in the aftermath, Hector turned his back on the White Tiger and gave the amulets to Blackbyrd, telling him to return them to the Sons of the Tiger.

In the period that followed, two others used the name White Tiger. One was a real white tiger given human form by the High Evolutionary, while the other was Kasper Cole, who took on the role briefly after using a Black Panther costume.

The call of the Amulets of Power proved too much for Hector, and a few years later he became White Tiger again. After trying to stop a robbery that involved the death of a police officer, Hector was found standing over the body and arrested. While Matt Murdock came to his defense and was about to get the charges dropped, Hector panicked and fled the courtroom, only to be gunned down by cops outside. The amulets were passed on to his niece, FBI agent Angela Del Toro.

Left: SPECTACULAR SPIDER-MAN #10 (SEP. 1977) White Tiger pursued Professor Vasquez after learning he had stolen an ancient manuscript, but Spider-Man believed White Tiger was the culprit.

Opposite: SPECTACULAR SPIDER-MAN #52 (MAR. 1981) White Tiger only barely survived Gideon Mace and his men shooting him and dumping his body outside the *Daily Bugle* newspaper offices.

Del Toro joined an FBI task force investigating Matt Murdock's links to Daredevil, hoping to work out what had motivated her uncle to become the White Tiger. After Matt offered her guidance on her newfound abilities, Angela quit her role in the FBI, and the two started to train together. Black Widow also took Del Toro under her wing and helped her find a suitable costume. When Angela realized that Sano Orii—a Yakuza operative who had once killed her partner in the NYPD—had been freed from jail, she uncovered links between him and Chaeyi, an organization that helped overthrow governments. Aided by Iron Fist, Luke Cage, Spider-Man, and Black Widow, White Tiger stopped their operations in New York.

Del Toro's skills soon attracted the attention of the ninja cult the Hand. Killed by Lady Bullseye, she was resurrected as one of their assassins, working closely with a corrupted Daredevil when he created his Shadowland in Hell's Kitchen. In the aftermath of Daredevil's defeat, Angela ended up in jail and the amulets were passed on to her aunt, Ava.

Ava, who had hero-worshiped her brother Hector, was selected by the A.I. Jocasta to be inducted into the Avengers Academy. She was described as talented, but intense, and felt obliged to honor the White Tiger legacy.

WHITE TIGER #2 (FEB. 2007)
Before becoming White Tiger, Angela Del Toro had been trained in martial arts by her Uncle Hector and "Uncle Danny"—aka Iron Fist.

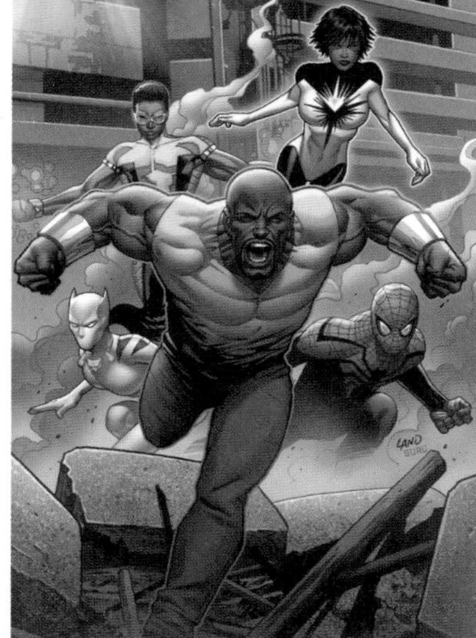

MIGHTY AVENGERS #1 (NOV. 2013) While part of Luke Cage's Avengers, Ava started a relationship with Victor Alvarez, aka Power Man.

MIGHTY AVENGERS #8 (MAY 2014) Ava was the first of the White Tigers to meet the Tiger God, though the increased power it gave her came at a great price.

Years before, she had been lucky to survive when Gideon Mace massacred her family. When fellow student Reptil was possessed by his future self, he helped an alien called Hybrid attack the Avengers Academy. White Tiger flew into a rage, fiercely attacking Reptil, only to pull back just before killing him.

Later at the school, when industrialist Jeremy Briggs sought to depower the world's superhumans, his agent Coat of Arms stole the power from Ava's amulets. Ava met the real power behind them—an ancient Tiger God, one of the first entities ancient people feared—and promised it free rein once a month if it granted her more power. The deity agreed, and a repowered Ava helped defeat Briggs and Coat of Arms.

Ava graduated shortly after, joining Luke Cage's Heroes for Hire before following him into his Avengers squad. While fighting the demon Shuma-Gorath, Power Man (Victor Alvarez) pulled chi from New Yorkers and passed it on to Ava, so she could attack the demon. The tiger entity inside her welcomed the influx of energy and struck, weakening the demon enough for the Avengers to defeat it.

Ava allowed the Tiger God to take control of her when her family's killer, Gideon Mace, was freed from jail. Ava tore through her teammates when they tried to stop her, with Spectrum using an energy blast to halt her. The Avengers took custody of Ava, and she made a deal with the Tiger God to give her control of its power again.

Ava faced another White Tiger when the Maker (an evil Reed Richards from a parallel Earth) sought to destroy the Avengers. He formed his own superteam, the New Revengers, and persuaded the imprisoned Angela Del Toro—Ava's niece, who was still under the influence of the Hand—to join them. The Maker gave Angela another amulet from a different dimension—one that was empowered by another Tiger God. When Angela confronted Ava, the two Tiger Gods merged and the new powerful entity then chose to pass on its power to Del Toro.

Ava continued as the White Tiger, but she now only had her martial arts prowess to rely on. Ava faced Angela again during a final confrontation between the Avengers and Revengers. She shattered Del Toro's amulet, destroying her connection to the Tiger god. Both aunt and niece decided to end their time as White Tigers, and felt sorry for the next person the deity would select as its avatar.

Not long after, Ava and Angela learned the Hand was using the Sons of the Tiger's old dojo as a base. It was enough to make them take up their White Tiger mantles again. Ava was then on hand when the Defenders called for help, and later became part of the Daughters of Liberty—an all-female group who had been covertly protecting American freedom for centuries. Ava helped them free Steve Rogers from jail and stop right-wing group the Watchdogs from killing immigrants crossing the border from Mexico.

Ava's actions proved that both she and Del Toro had made the right decision. They would continue Hector's legacy with or without the amulets. They would both be White Tigers.

NEW AVENGERS #7 (APR. 2016) Ava fought with a possessed Angela, who was still under the malign influence of the Hand. After smashing Angela's amulet, Ava finally managed to free her neice.

"I don't need weapons. I *am* a weapon."

ANGELA DEL TORO

SHADOWS AND LIGHT

DAREDEVIL

THE MAN WITHOUT FEAR

Matt Murdock is Daredevil, hero of Hell's Kitchen, New York. Matt became a masked vigilante following the murder of his father, "Battlin'" Jack Murdock. By then, Matt was already a highly skilled fighter. He had lost his sight as a young boy, saving a blind man from being hit by a truck carrying radioactive chemicals. The accident took Matt's vision, but enhanced his other senses. It also gave Matt a kind of radar sense that helped him move smoothly through the world around him. Taking the name Daredevil, Matt operated as a crime-fighting hero as well as establishing himself as a partner in a law firm. He honed his martial arts skills with the help of a ninja master named Stick. Also blind, Stick was leader of the Chaste, a secret cabal of martial artists sworn to oppose the evil of the Hand—the world's deadliest ninja assassins. Originally, Stick hoped Matt might one day join the Chaste and succeed him as its leader, but following the death of Matt's father, it became clear that Matt had too much rage inside him, and was battling too many inner demons, to truly be a member of the mystical Chaste.

Daredevil has faced off against some of the world's most dangerous villains, including the deadly hired killer Bullseye, the mind-controlling Purple Man, New York crime-lord Wilson Fisk (better known as the Kingpin), and the great love of his life, Elektra, the ninja assassin. Matt has also battled his inner demons, but no matter how far he has fallen, he has always managed to get back up to fight again. He has faced those demons and defeated them. Daredevil really is the Man Without Fear.

DAREDEVIL #28 (DEC. 2017) Matt Murdock is an exceptional mixed martial artist, who utilizes ninja techniques and his own boxing skills. Both are enhanced by his amazing radar sense, helping him take on ninja assassins and Super Villains.

The Man in Black

Matt Murdock is Daredevil, one of the greatest martial artists in the world; a blind Super Hero trained by a ninja master.

Matt's father was "Battlin'" Jack Murdock, a boxer from Hell's Kitchen. Jack had been strong-armed into working for local gangster Roscoe Sweeney, aka the Fixer, though he kept this part of his life from his young son. Matt's mother had left home to become a nun shortly after he was born, leaving Jack to raise Matt alone, though Jack told the boy she had died. While Matt hero-worshiped his father, Jack didn't want his son following in his own violent footsteps—so much so, that he once flew into a rage and struck Matt when he learned his son had been in a fight.

Left: DAREDEVIL: THE MAN WITHOUT FEAR #1 (OCT. 1993)
Stick's harsh training methods helped Matt come to terms with the loss of his sight and learn how to use his new abilities

Opposite left: DAREDEVIL: THE MAN WITHOUT FEAR #1 (OCT. 1993)
Having promised his father he would not get into fights, the young Matt would sneak into the gym late at night and practice in secret.

This act made the young Matt realize that laws were needed to protect the weak, and he set his mind on a life as a lawyer. Matt's studious ways made him a target for bullies at school, but he never responded when they taunted his passivity by calling him "daredevil." Instead, late at night he would sneak into the gym his father used and take his anger out on the punching bags.

When still young, Matt was caught in a terrible accident that changed his life. When he saw an out-of-control truck which was carrying chemicals about to hit an old, blind man, Matt dived to push the man out the way. While the truck missed them, one of the chemical canisters cracked open, blinding Matt with a strange radioactive substance.

As he recovered in hospital, Matt realized that although he was blind, his other senses had been heightened way beyond those of a normal human being. He had also gained a radar sense that "showed" Matt the world around him in his mind's eye. Stick, a ninja master who belonged to a group called the Chaste, aided Matt's recovery by training him, teaching him his unique style of martial arts, and helping Matt make the most of his new abilities.

DAREDEVIL: THE MAN WITHOUT FEAR #5 (FEB. 1994) When Daredevil fought to save a kidnapped girl, he had his first run-in with thugs working for Wilson Fisk, the Kingpin of Crime.

Matt continued to lead a double life. Under Stick's guidance, he sharpened his fighting skills and learned to optimize his radar sense—he could now fire arrows and hit a bullseye every time just by using his other senses. He also continued his studies at college, making a lifelong friend in fellow student Foggy Nelson. When Matt's father was told to throw a fight by the Fixer, Jack was going to obey, until he saw Matt at the side of the ring. He couldn't throw the fight in front of his son. Jack won by a knockout, losing the Fixer a lot of money. The Fixer and his men gunned down Jack as punishment.

Seeking revenge, Matt donned a mask and set out to bring the Fixer's crew to justice. He hunted them down until only the Fixer and his driver remained. When Matt confronted the Fixer, the mobster died of a heart attack. Along the way, Matt took the name the school bullies had once called him: Daredevil. Matt's act of revenge had repercussions, however. Stick refused to teach him anymore, believing that Matt was too wild to become one of the Chaste.

Matt continued to fight crime as Daredevil while setting up a law practice with Foggy. When a young girl was kidnapped, Matt donned black to save her. It resulted in Stick meeting him briefly and telling him not to get cocky. For Matt, it was a sign that he was on the right path. Daredevil made Hell's Kitchen his own. He created a costume based on an old outfit his father had briefly worn when fighting as "the Devil."

The new hero also started to face some strange foes—such as criminal mastermind the Owl and the deluded Melvin Potter, aka the Gladiator, a costume-maker obsessed with the ideals of the Roman arena. All through it, Matt used the skills his sensei had taught him. He might not have become one of the Chaste, but as Daredevil, Matt had become a Super Hero.

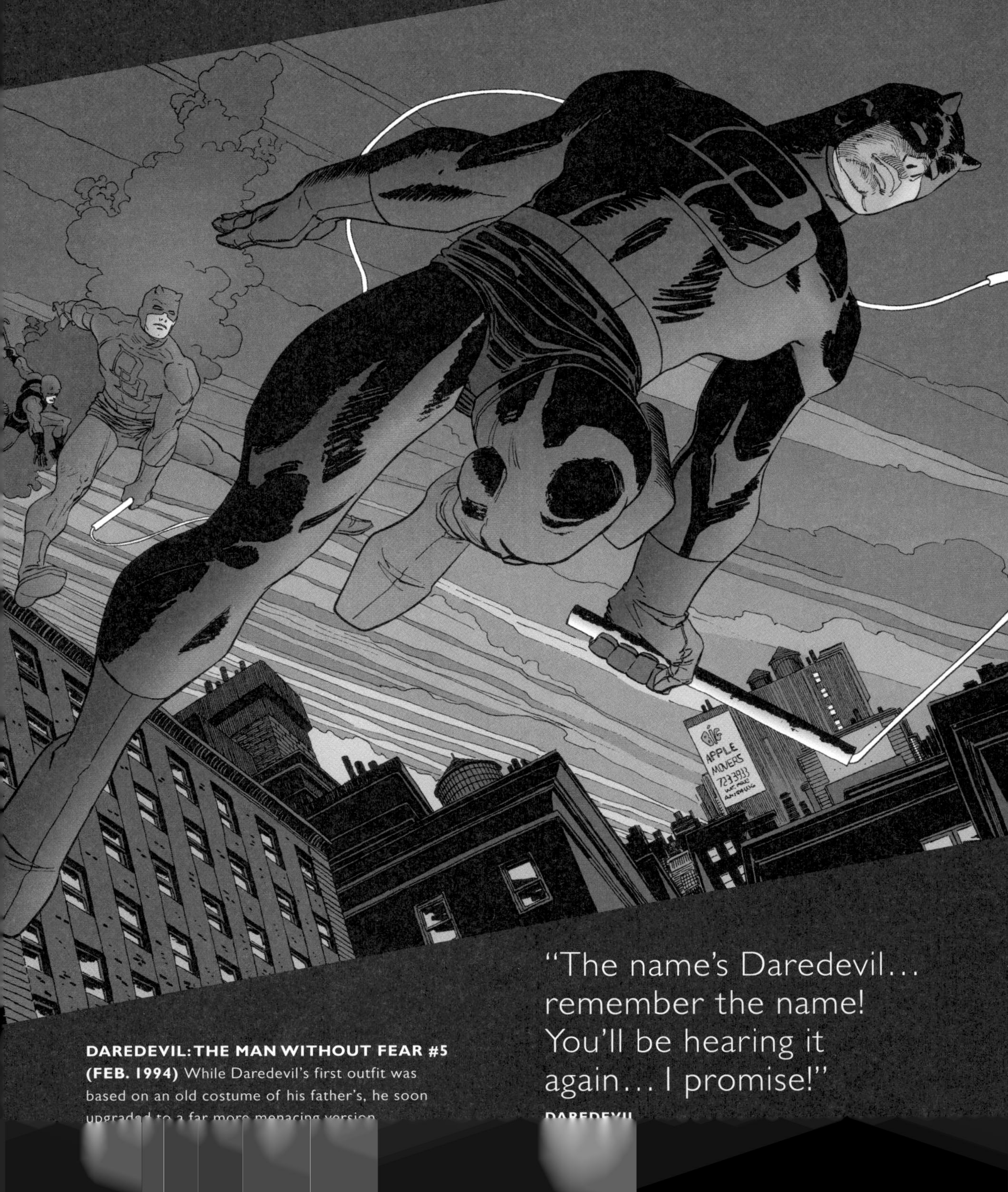

DAREDEVIL: THE MAN WITHOUT FEAR #5 (FEB. 1994) While Daredevil's first outfit was based on an old costume of his father's, he soon upgraded to a far more menacing version.

"The name's Daredevil… remember the name! You'll be hearing it again… I promise!"

DAREDEVIL

The Chaste

A founding member of the Hand, Master Izo left the ninja cult when he realized it was becoming corrupted. He established rival martial arts clan the Chaste, with the intention for it to become a force for justice.

The Chaste built its temple home on top of a mountain in China. Adepts were challenged to climb "the Wall"—an impossibly high ice cliff—to reach their base. Few made it. Many of the Chaste have developed special skills through their training, including the ability to silently communicate with each other via telepathy.

Master Izo was eventually thrown out of the Chaste by Stick and other members when his drinking and gambling became too much. Both Daredevil Matt Murdock and the deadly ninja Elektra were seen as potential modern-day recruits, but both were deemed unworthy and too wild. Years later, Stick helped Matt regain his radar sense when he briefly lost it, and after Elektra's death, turned to Daredevil for help when the Hand tried to wipe out the Chaste once and for all. Stick called a meeting of the Seven—the Chaste's greatest warriors—but only three arrived in New York, the others seemingly killed en route.

Above: DAREDEVIL #113 (JAN. 2009) Master Izo had spent centuries fighting the Hand. He spotted the potential in a young Matt Murdock and recommended him to Stick.

"You're in for a real fight, punk. You might not survive it."

STICK

Above and left: DAREDEVIL #187 (OCT. 1982) As leader of the Chaste, Stick was trained in the use of various weapons, but preferred to use his staff.

Those who did make it each had special skills. Stone was Stick's second-in-command. He was trained to be able to withstand any attack—if he knew an attack was coming. Shaft was an expert archer, and Claw was gifted with the use of tekko-kagi, a bladed weapon favored by many ninjas.

Stick and the Chaste managed to defeat the Hand's greatest killer—Kirigi—but after traveling to Matt's apartment with Daredevil and the Black Widow, they were attacked by a legion of assassins. Claw was the first to fall. Outnumbered, Stick realized they faced certain death and made the ultimate sacrifice. Using an arcane ability, Stick and Shaft took the life force of the assassins around them, as Stone protected Daredevil and Black Widow. Stick and Shaft's bodies couldn't contain the energy of the ninjas, and they died. Stone was now the last member of the Seven.

When the Hand later tried to bring Elektra back to life, Stone gave his own life force to complete the process, ensuring she returned purified. Following her resurrection, Elektra journeyed to the Chaste's home to come to terms with her rebirth, while Daredevil continued his fight against the Hand, the group of assassins he would one day lead.

Left: DAREDEVIL #189 (DEC. 1982) The Chaste's control of chi was so great they could both give and take life from others—but only at great cost to themselves.

Right: DAREDEVIL #190 (JAN. 1983) Following the death of Stick, Stone helped Daredevil prevent the Hand from bringing Elektra back from the dead as one of their deadly assassins.

The Devil's Foes

While the Hand was one of Daredevil's most persistent enemies, others presented just as great a threat. Some, such as Wilson Fisk, came close to destroying Daredevil more than once.

New York's Kingpin of Crime, Fisk has always found Daredevil one of his biggest threats. Despite his huge size, Fisk is a master martial artist trained in a variety of styles, including sumo wrestling, and uses them in such a way as to make them work with his bulk and strength. He regularly trains against leading martial artists, often leaving broken or dead bodies in his wake.

For the most part, though, Fisk prefers for others to do his killing—hired hands like Bullseye and Elektra. Bullseye proved to be especially deadly in Fisk's employ, and helped him increase his control of the New York crime scene. Likewise, when the Kingpin learned that Matt Murdock and Daredevil were actually one and the same, he manipulated his connections in the US military to unleash Nuke—a deranged modern-day take on Captain America—on the Man Without Fear.

The Kingpin has utilized other deadly martial artists in his war against Daredevil, such as Maya Lopez, aka Echo, whom he helped raise after ordering the execution of her father. Able to mimic any action she sees, Maya became an expert ballet dancer and martial artist. Fisk brought her up to hate Daredevil, only for Maya to eventually learn the truth and turn on Fisk to become a hero.

Left and top inset: DAREDEVIL #100 (OCT. 2007) Daredevil has amassed a small army of deadly enemies. One attack by Mister Fear left the hero believing he was under attack from all of them.

Fisk also sent the mentally unstable mutant Typhoid Mary after Daredevil. Mary's fractured personalities range from the nice to the deadly, some having abilities such as pyrokinesis. Sometimes deranged, Mary still has a love-hate relationship with Daredevil and chose to stand by his side when he gained control of the Hand.

Daredevil's other enemies have ranged from the Purple Man—who can control the minds of those nearby—and Mister Fear—who uses a special gas to create terror in his victims—through to Mephisto and his son Blackheart, who have been rulers of Hell. He has also faced villains who normally plague other heroes, such as Spider-Man's enemy Mysterio. The special-effects genius concocted a mad scenario that left Daredevil believing he was taking care of a baby who was either the Messiah reborn or the Anti-Christ. Mysterio wanted Daredevil to kill him, but Daredevil resisted, leading to the villain taking his own life.

If those closest to Matt were asked who his deadliest enemy was, they might say himself. Daredevil has a habit of self-destruction, perhaps best illustrated by his takeover of the Hand...

Above: DAREDEVIL #46 (JUN. 2003) Typhoid Mary became obsessed with Daredevil. The hero had nearly killed her during one of his first outings.

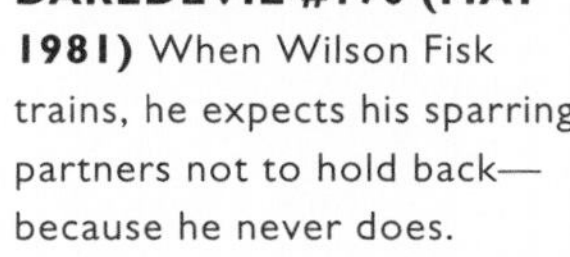

DAREDEVIL #170 (MAY 1981) When Wilson Fisk trains, he expects his sparring partners not to hold back—because he never does.

Shadowland

The Hand was searching for a new leader and Daredevil's grandmaster, Master Izo, had a plan. This was an opportunity to destroy the ninja cabal once and for all—with Daredevil's help.

For his part, Matt was again plagued by guilt. This time as a result of his failure to prevent Bullseye blowing up a building and killing all but one of its residents (only Victor Alvarez, the new Power Man, survived). When Wilson Fisk, the Kingpin, tried to become the Hand's new leader, Daredevil stepped forward and agreed to lead the clan. There was one flaw in his plan, however. To be initiated as leader, Matt first had to kill Master Izo. Daredevil executed him with one punch—the Man Without Fear was now the leader of the world's deadliest assassins.

In fact, Izo survived—Matt had only pretended to kill him. The master ninja had slowed his own heartbeat so he appeared dead, and was later revived by Black Tarantula. While Izo still wanted to bring down the Hand, Daredevil was starting to have other ideas. Norman Osborn's dark reign—where he had replaced S.H.I.E.L.D. with his own H.A.M.M.E.R. organization—was nearing its end, but the villain still held power. When Osborn's minions approached Hell's Kitchen, the Kingpin saw an opportunity to sit back and watch his foes fight, and used Lady Bullseye to provoke violence between H.A.M.M.E.R. and the Hand. In the aftermath, H.A.M.M.E.R.'s forces disappeared—taken to an underground prison created on the orders of Daredevil, who proclaimed that Hell's Kitchen was now under the Hand's control.

Daredevil used the Hand's resources to build a huge base—Shadowland—on the site of the building Bullseye had earlier destroyed. He also issued an edict asking for other heroes to come to his side, but added a menacing threat that they were either with him, or against him. Daredevil also settled an old score. When Bullseye broke free from a prison van, Daredevil set the Hand on him. Luke Cage and Iron Fist could only watch as members of the Hand weakened Bullseye, and Daredevil killed him, running him through with the blade of his sai.

Opposite and above: SHADOWLAND #1 (SEP. 2010) While Bullseye killed several Hand assassins that attacked him, he was no match for a vengeful Daredevil. Matt dislocated both of Bullseye's shoulders before killing him with a sai, echoing Bullseye's killing of Elektra years before.

Above: SHADOWLAND #3 (NOV. 2010) Any hope Iron Fist and his allies had of talking sense into Daredevil was dashed when a separate attack by Ghost Rider brought a furious response from the Man Without Fear.

Matt's friends Iron Fist, Luke Cage, Colleen Wing, Misty Knight, and Shang-Chi met with Daredevil and tried to make him to see the error of his ways. Shortly before, Fisk had gained the Black Scroll, an ancient Hand rite that gave him control of the Spirit of Vengeance—Ghost Rider—who attacked Shadowland just as the heroes made their case. Convinced it was all part of an organized attack, Daredevil ordered the Hand to kill his old allies. Spider-Man offered assistance in the fight, but they were helplessly outnumbered. Fortunately, the Punisher blasted his way into Shadowland, allowing them a route of escape.

As the heroes regrouped, Izo explained that he had failed. Rather than turn the Hand into a force for good, the Hand had corrupted Matt into a force for evil. The Hand really belonged to Clan Snakeroot, an inner cabal that worshiped the Beast—a demon that fed off violence and death. Daredevil was now possessed by the Beast.

Daredevil had his loyal soldiers Black Tarantula and White Tiger by his side—not realizing that Black Tarantula was really an agent of Master Izo. Typhoid Mary and Elektra had also joined him. As the Beast's control of Matt grew, evil emanated out from Shadowland, bringing violence to Hell's Kitchen. The more people turned to violence, the stronger the Beast became.

The heroes had one last desperate plan. Elektra had only joined Matt to help her allies gain entrance to Shadowland. Iron Fist and his allies returned—with Wolverine added to their ranks—to try and save Daredevil, or kill him. To make the situation graver, Daredevil had retrieved Bullseye's corpse and decided to use the Hand's

Above: SHADOWLAND #2 (OCT. 2010) As Daredevil led the Hand, the influence of the Beast became ever greater—eventually starting to mutate his body.

arcane rites to raise him from the dead so he could become their new champion.

As the heroes fought Daredevil, the Beast started to gain more power and strength—even surviving Wolverine's claws. When all seemed lost, Izo and Iron Fist confronted Daredevil. Danny Rand used all his power to punch his former ally. The Beast mocked Iron Fist, saying a mere punch couldn't kill him. But Danny hadn't punched Daredevil to hurt him, he had done it to heal him. Within Matt's subconscious, Matt faced down his own demons. Realizing he had been used by the Beast, Daredevil ritually stabbed himself, ending the demon's control. In the aftermath, the Hand melted away and White Tiger was imprisoned.

With Elektra's help, Matt survived and escaped Shadowland. He found himself in an old church, where he asked for forgiveness before leaving to find his path to redemption. Fisk proved to be the true victor. Typhoid Mary had been working for him all along and brought the Hand to his side. Fisk was now not just the Kingpin of Crime but also leader of the Hand… and before too long, he would also be the Mayor of New York.

"There is no Murdock. There is only the Beast!"

DAREDEVIL

Right: SHADOWLAND #5 (JAN. 2011) Iron Fist used the power of his chi to disrupt the Beast's control of Matt, helping the hero regain control—albeit with tragic results.

Battle for New York

After a short time living in San Francisco and revealing his secret identity to the world, Matt returned to New York. Daredevil's true persona was once again in place thanks to the actions of the mind-controlling Purple Children. When Matt had saved them from their evil father, they had repaid him by making everyone on Earth forget that Matt was Daredevil. It caused some problems for Matt, however. Elektra thought Daredevil and Matt were different people, as did Foggy until Matt told him what had happened.

Back in New York, Matt worked as the Assistant District Attorney. As Daredevil, Matt also gained a sidekick—a young Chinese hero called Blindspot. Sam Chung had made a special suit that rendered him invisible and used it to fight crime. Matt started to train Sam, but became concerned about a cult leader called Tenfingers who led "The Church of the Sheltering Hands" in Chinatown. One of Tenfingers' enforcers was Lu Wei, Sam's mother. Tenfingers had gained his power by stealing dark magic from the Hand. When the Hand came to reclaim its power, Daredevil and Blindspot were caught up in the conflict. They saved members of the cult, but Tenfingers was killed.

DAREDEVIL #1 (FEB. 2016)
Daredevil started to train new hero Blindspot. The teen was a Chinese gymnast who had been brought to America by his mother.

Shortly after, Daredevil found himself fighting an Inhuman serial killer called Muse. The villain killed and reshaped his victims, leaving them as gruesome works of art. When Daredevil asked the Inhumans for help, the Man Without Fear ended up fighting Karnak, and bettering the Inhuman martial artist. Muse was finally caught and taken into custody by the Inhumans—but only after he had captured Blindspot and taken his eyes, leaving Matt's new student blind. Feeling guilty, Matt turned to his local priest for guidance and learned that Father Jordan was actually a member of the Ordo Draconum, or Order of the Dragon, an ancient sect of Catholic warrior priests formed way back in the 15th century.

Sam's mother, Lu Wei, made a deal with the Hand to restore her son's vision. When Blindspot contacted Matt asking for help, Matt tracked his ex-student to a Hand temple in China—only to find it was a trap. Sam's mother had offered her soul to the Beast of the Hand in return for it restoring her son's eyesight. However, her son had gone one better and offered the Beast Daredevil's soul instead.

The Beast kept Daredevil prisoner for weeks, trying to break him. As the demon tortured Daredevil, Sam and his mother were allowed to leave. When Sam heard his former mentor's screams he realized the mistake he had made and returned to try to help Matt. Blindspot and Daredevil were facing certain death until Lu Wei tried to intervene. The Beast grabbed Sam's mother and consumed her soul before vanishing, teleporting away with the temple, leaving Sam and Matt alone on an empty mountain.

Daredevil had a shock waiting for him on his return to New York. Wilson Fisk had become Mayor. One of Fisk's first acts was to outlaw Super Heroes. Much to Matt's surprise, Fisk offered him the job of Deputy Mayor. The crime lord intended to sideline Matt so he could not interfere with his greater plans to dominate New York and become a true Kingpin. Muse had also returned, but was now using street art to torment Fisk. When Blindspot confronted Muse, the Beast of the Hand offered Sam more power if he turned to darkness and killed the Inhuman. Sam accepted, but then refused to kill Muse.

DAREDEVIL #600 (MAY 2018) With the Hand attacking New York, Daredevil called on his old friends to defend the city. Echo, Misty Knight, Spider-Man, Moon Knight, Iron Fist, Luke Cage, and Jessica Jones joined him.

When Daredevil assembled his allies to try to take down Fisk and his new cartel, Iron Fist, Luke Cage, Echo, Moon Knight, Spider-Man, and Jessica Jones were all arrested. At the same time, the Hand returned to New York en masse and attacked Fisk, leaving him grievously injured.

Above: DAREDEVIL #600 (MAY 2018) Wilson Fisk's plans to dominate the New York criminal underworld were shattered when a secret meeting with other crime bosses was attacked by the Hand, leaving Fisk close to death.

With Fisk close to death, Matt took over as Mayor. Realizing the city was under siege from the Hand, he ordered the release of the heroes and put them to work fighting the ninja cult. The Hand's warriors were spreading throughout the city and the Beast's strength was increasing the more people feared events. Eventually it breathed out, spreading its evil through the streets of New York.

Help came from an unexpected source—the Order of the Dragon, led by Father Jordan, came to their aid, allowing Daredevil to take the fight to the Hand. The ninja cult wanted Blindspot—and while the hero was willing to sacrifice himself to keep the peace, Police Commissioner Nalini Karnik refused to let him do so. Fortunately, Daredevil and his allies arrived in time to save them, Daredevil using a sword given to him by Father Jordan to vanquish the Beast.

Fisk recovered and reclaimed his role as Mayor, but cut a deal with Matt to repeal the law outlawing Super Heroes, while Sam was offered a place in the Order of the Dragon. It was time for Matt to make a fresh start. He tried to turn his back on his alter ego, but soon found it calling to him. Hell's Kitchen still needed a protector—it still needed Daredevil.

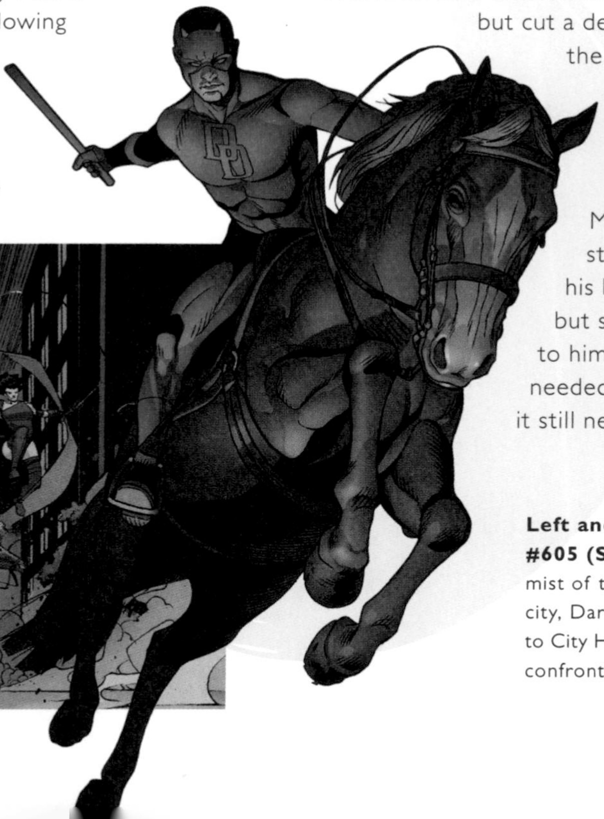

Left and far left: DAREDEVIL #605 (SEP. 2018) As the green mist of the Beast threatened the city, Daredevil and his allies rushed to City Hall to save Blindspot and confront the evil entity.

"I will fight. Forever. For everyone, whether they know it or not."

DAREDEVIL

ELEKTRA

NINJA ASSASSIN

Elektra is one of the world's deadliest assassins. The daughter of a Greek ambassador, Elektra's life has always been tainted by violence. From the murder of her mother, shot just before she gave birth to Elektra, to the death of her father while she was at college, life left a darkness in Elektra, one that could only be eased by violence. A black belt by the age of 12, at college she slipped away into the night to find trouble, taking her anger out on criminals she deemed worthy of punishment. Following the death of her father, she left her lover, Matt Murdock, and tried to join the Chaste—a group of elite ninjas sworn to fight the evil Hand—but after a year of training she was deemed unworthy and ordered to leave. She planned to infiltrate the Hand to prove herself worthy of the Chaste, but the Hand turned her into its own deadly assassin.

Elektra became a dark legend, a killer who other killers feared to mention. When she left the Hand, she went freelance, traveling the world in pursuit of targets, her reputation increasing with each kill. When she met Matt Murdock once again, the darkness started to lift. Despite her cold-blooded reputation, she found herself saving his life time after time. She died in Matt's arms—a victim of Daredevil's archenemy, Bullseye. She was later reborn, purified thanks to the powers of Daredevil and Stone of the Chaste. However, Elektra was later forced to embrace her own darkness to save others, and returned to her murderous ways.

Now, while she remains an assassin, she is trying to come to terms with the darkness within her. She has survived death itself and fears neither man nor beast. No wonder Elektra is a legend among killers.

ELEKTRA #1 (APR. 2017) Trained by the Chaste and the Hand, Elektra has proven to be one of the world's deadliest assassins—though at times she has also used her abilities for good, both as an agent of S.H.I.E.L.D. and a freelance operative.

Shadows of Death

The origins of the Hand stretch back to a time of great bloodshed: 16th-century Japan.

The Hand's founder was Kagenobu Yoshioka. The organization was created as a force for good, albeit a nationalistic one; fighting against the influx of foreign merchants entering the country and the corrupt daimyo (feudal lords) who ruled the land. Yoshioka's mother claimed he was the son of a samurai who had died in battle. With his father dead, Yoshioka and his mother fell on hard times. When a Portuguese merchant attacked his mother,

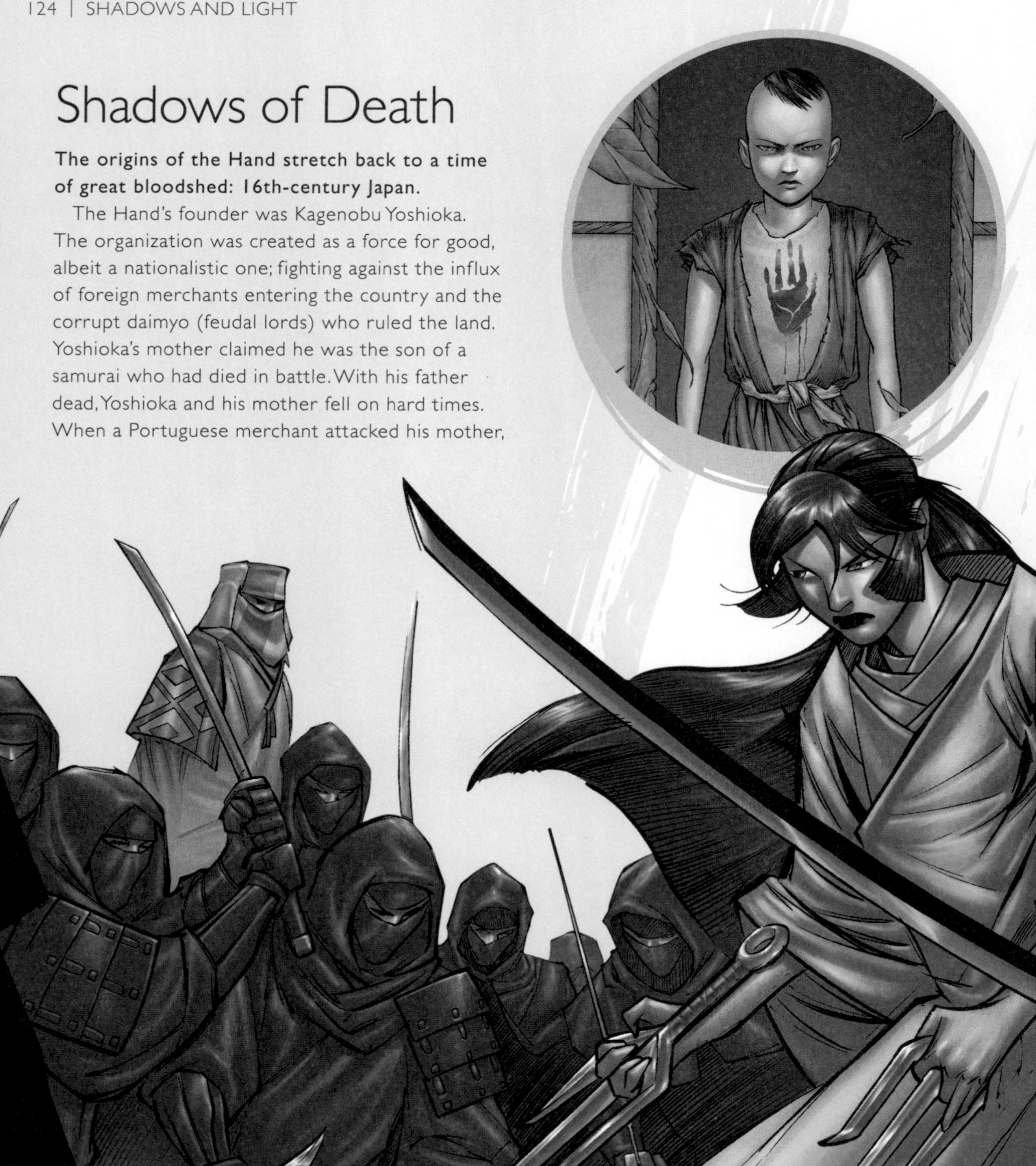

Opposite: ELEKTRA: THE HAND #1 (NOV. 2004) The young Kagenobu Yoshioka was left with the bloody handprint of his mother on his top following her arrest. It was a print that would inspire the creation of the Hand.

Below: ELEKTRA: THE HAND #5 (FEB. 2005) Kagenobu Yoshioka and Eliza Martinez were prepared for death—but for Eliza even death was no escape from the Hand.

the young Yoshioka killed him. Realizing it could mean her son's execution, his mother claimed responsibility and was arrested by the authorities. As she was dragged away, Yoshioka's mother stretched out her arm, leaving a bloody handprint on her son's top. In the aftermath, Yoshioka was taken in by a sympathetic teacher named Saburo Ishiyama and taught the ways of the samurai.

In time, Yoshioka became a ronin, wandering the land seeking worthy causes. He remained a nationalist with a deep hatred of foreigners. When Ishiyama died, Yoshioka was called home and asked to take over Ishiyama's school. He agreed, and asked an old rival, Sasaki, to help him. Yoshioka then recruited leaders from the other islands of Japan and claimed the five islands were like the five digits of a hand—stronger together. Yoshioka planned to use the Hand to attack traders and overthrow the corrupt regime.

When Yoshioka took on a female student—the half-Japanese Eliza Martinez—dissent began to grow. Yoshioka and Eliza became close, but when they learned Sasaki was taking the school down a darker path—one where its members were willing to become paid assassins—they opposed the change. Yoshioka killed Sasaki in a duel, only to be confronted by the rest of the Hand and its leaders. Eliza and Yoshioka fought valiantly, but soon realized they were facing certain death. Not wanting to be killed by the enemy, Yoshioka asked his lover to kill him. Once she had completed her grim task, she took her own life. The Hand then used dark magic to bring Eliza back from the dead to fight as one of its brainwashed warriors.

"Tonight the Hand has been unleashed on the world!"

KAGENOBU YOSHIOKA

Left: DAREDEVIL #26 (NOV. 2017) The Beast of the Hand was a being of exceptional power that could feed off the pain, suffering, and anger of the world around it.

Above: DAREDEVIL #5 (MAY 2016) Sent by the Hand to kill the Chinatown crime boss Tenfingers—himself a former member of the Hand—the Fist easily tore through his guards.

Master Izo was one of the founding members of the Hand, but when he saw the dark path the organization was taking, he left to create the Chaste, a group sworn to oppose the Hand's evil. The Hand had been taken over by the Snakeroot Clan, who worshiped an ancient demon known only as the Beast. It is from the Beast that many of the Hand's members supposedly gain their powers. Some of the Hand's number have sorcerous abilities and can bring the dead back to life. At times, they have killed heroes such as Wolverine and put them through one of their ancient rites so they would be reborn as assassins under the Hand's control. The clan has other undead creatures working for it, such as the Fist—a sentient corpse created by one hundred members of the Hand sacrificing their lives.

World War II saw the Hand expanding to become a global force. The clan worked with Nazi leader Baron von Strucker and the Lupine villain Romulus in Madripoor, only to come into conflict with Captain America and Wolverine. It also helped form the modern incarnation of Hydra before Baron von Strucker purged the Hand from the terrorist organization.

Over the decades, the Hand has included some of the deadliest killers in the world and has resurrected some to obey its commands. Kirigi was one of the Hand's greatest assassins and according to legend, he couldn't be killed. He was called into action to assassinate Elektra and could kill three members of the Hand with just one stroke of his blade. Elektra eventually managed to kill him by beheading him. He was later revived only for Stick and the Chaste to defeat him, this time burning his corpse. Mutants such as Psylocke, Sabretooth, and Omega Red have all been part of the Hand at various times, however it is arguably Elektra who remains the deadliest killer ever to have been a member.

The daughter of Greek ambassador Hugo Natchios, Elektra never met her mother—she was shot while pregnant and died shortly after giving birth to Elektra. A troubled child, Elektra

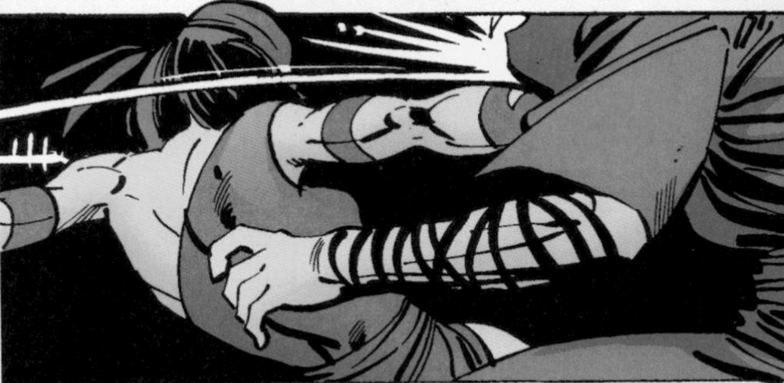

Top right: DAREDEVIL #175 (OCT. 1981) The Hand made several attempts to kill Elektra after she left, including sending Kirigi, their greatest warrior. All failed.

Below right: DAREDEVIL #190 (JAN. 1983) While first trying to infiltrate the Hand, Elektra was tricked by the assassins into killing her own sensei.

discovered martial arts at an early age and gained her black belt by the age of 12. While at Columbia University, Elektra met Matt Murdock and the two had an intense relationship.

When Elektra and her father were taken hostage by terrorists, a disguised Matt rescued them only for police outside to open fire and accidentally kill Elektra's father. The death sent Elektra down a dark path. Her sensei suggested she contact the Chaste, and at first Elektra thought she'd found a home with the elite martial artists, but Stick sensed a darkness within her and asked her to leave. Hoping to prove herself worthy of the Chaste, Elektra infiltrated the Hand. Tricked by the evil organization into killing her own sensei, Elektra was broken and soon molded into becoming one of its greatest killers.

While she eventually broke away from the Hand, Elektra remained an assassin. It was a path that would one day lead her back to New York and to her first love, Matt Murdock.

Left, above and below: **DAREDEVIL #174 (SEP. 1981)** When the Hand targeted Matt Murdock and the Gladiator, Elektra came to their aid—but with Matt's extra senses out of action, he was unaware of his guardian angel.

Death and Resurrection

After leaving the Hand, Elektra became a freelance assassin. She managed to stop Ken Wind—a politician linked to the Beast—from becoming President, but this brought her to the attention of spy agency S.H.I.E.L.D.

Elektra eventually returned to New York to assassinate a thief called Alarich Wallenquist who was protected by mobster Eric Slaughter. While hunting her target, Elektra crossed paths with Daredevil for the first time since her relationship with Matt had ended. When Slaughter's men captured Elektra, Daredevil helped her get free—though he then took Elektra's target with him.

A short while later, Elektra was hunting an assignment in Paris when her target was killed by the Hand. Following the assassins, she learned they had a new target: Matt Murdock. Elektra traveled to New York and protected Matt from the Hand. After saving Matt, the Hand made Elektra its next target. The assignment was given to Kirigi—one of the Hand's greatest killers—although he proved no match for Elektra. When Wilson Fisk became aware of Elektra's exceptional skills, he offered her a job. Elektra accepted, but when Fisk ordered Elektra to take on a new target, Foggy Nelson, it brought back old memories. At the same time, Bullseye had

DAREDEVIL #181 (APR. 1982) After Bullseye landed a killing blow on Elektra, he followed her as she stumbled away and witnessed her final moments in Matt Murdock's arms.

"I've seen you before... in college. You were Matt's girl... Elektra."

FOGGY NELSON

escaped from prison and hoped to prove his worth to Fisk by killing Elektra. As Elektra was about to assassinate the lawyer, he recognized her as "Matt's girl..." and Elektra let her target go. Shortly after, Bullseye attacked her. A vicious fight ensued that ended when he slit Elektra's throat with a playing card and then impaled her with one of her own sai. Elektra died in Matt's arms. Daredevil eventually defeated Bullseye, but was left traumatized by the loss of his first love.

A few months later, members of the Hand stole Elektra's corpse, hoping to resurrect her and make her one of their own again. Daredevil, Black Widow, and Stone attacked the Hand as they started the rite. When Daredevil saw Elektra's body, he tried to bring her back to life. He failed, but Stone realized that Daredevil had managed to purify Elektra; Stone then gave his own life force to resurrect her. Elektra was back, but Daredevil did not know she had been reborn. Elektra left New York and returned to the Chaste's wall, this time successfully climbing it before spending time at the martial arts enclave, recovering from her rebirth.

Left: DAREDEVIL #190 (JAN. 1983) Following her resurrection, Elektra returned to the Chaste. Purified of her inner darkness, she trained with them until she was drawn back to help Daredevil.

Years later, the Hand used its sorcery to create an assassin from the darkness that had been purified from Elektra. This darkness took on the form of Erynys, who knew all of Elektra's moves. When Erynys attacked Daredevil, Elektra returned to help defeat her—taking in her darkness to become one with it again. It also meant that she was no longer able to be one of the Chaste, and again found herself alone, reverting to life as an assassin.

When the Hand started to capture Super Heroes and transform them into assassins, Elektra was employed by S.H.I.E.L.D. to infiltrate the operation. A few months later, when the Avengers traveled to Japan to rescue Echo—Maya Lopez—they were confronted by Elektra leading the Hand. Maya killed Elektra, whose corpse transformed into that of a Skrull.

Several months earlier, a Skrull named Siri had been trained to replace Elektra, but when she tried to do so, Elektra had killed her. More Skrulls attacked. Overpowered, Elektra had been captured by the Skrulls and replaced by Pagon, who used Elektra's reputation to take over the Hand. Following the failure of the Skrull invasion, the real Elektra was freed from Skrull captivity, but placed in S.H.I.E.L.D. custody. When industrialist Norman Osborn took over S.H.I.E.L.D. and transformed it into H.A.M.M.E.R., he learned that the Skrulls had experimented on, and tortured, Elektra as they tried to find out the secrets of her revival.

Below left: NEW AVENGERS #31 (AUG. 2007) The Elektra killed by Echo was revealed to be a Skrull impostor, sent to sow seeds of distrust among Earth's heroes.

Elektra escaped from H.A.M.M.E.R. when the mercenary Paladin failed to assassinate her.

On the run, Elektra found herself hunted by Bullseye—now in the guise of Hawkeye. This time, Elektra got the better of the killer and left him severely wounded. Elektra learned that the contract on her had been taken out by vengeful S.H.I.E.L.D. agents who had survived a Helicarrier crash she had caused while undercover. Elektra escaped her would-be assassins but was alone again, although soon she would find herself working as part of a team filled with killers: the Thunderbolts.

Put together by Thunderbolt Ross when he was the Red Hulk, the Thunderbolts had one mission agenda: to take out criminals that regular heroes couldn't touch. To this end, Ross brought Elektra together with Venom (Flash Thompson), the Punisher, and Deadpool. While with the team, Elektra found herself facing-off against her older brother Orestez Natchios—who she thought was long dead—when he was found to be a terrorist leader. After a failed attempt on his part to kill the Thunderbolts, Orestze was supposedly executed by Elektra. However, sensing that Elektra hadn't done it, the Punisher—who had started a brief relationship with Elektra—tracked down Orestze and killed him. The Thunderbolts wasn't the only team Elektra helped out.

DARK REIGN: ELEKTRA #4 (AUG. 2009)
On the run from H.A.M.M.E.R., Elektra confronted Bullseye, at the time masquerading as Hawkeye, and left the assassin close to death.

Above: SAVAGE AVENGERS #5 (NOV. 2019)
As part of the "Savage Avengers," Elektra found herself facing assassins and killers pulled from across time.

When the Hand tried to resurrect the Hulk in Japan, Elektra fought alongside the mutant Rogue and the Avengers Unity Squad to try to stop the ritual taking place. Although they failed, Elektra was instrumental in stopping the reborn Hulk killing thousands and helped transport him to Brother Voodoo, who managed to cleanse him of the Hand's dark sorcery.

The villainous Hand remained Elektra's greatest enemy and she found herself fighting against its members with an unlikely team of Savage Avengers, whose number included Brother Voodoo, the Punisher, Venom, and a time-displaced Conan. Elektra soon learned that the ancient sorcerer Kulan Gath had allied with the Hand, intending to capture heroes and then sacrifice them to try to summon a malevolent god. Although they defeated the wizard, he escaped, giving Elektra a dangerous new enemy to track.

After the mind-controlling Purple Children wiped knowledge of Daredevil's secret identity from the world, they also altered Elektra's memory of her affair with Matt. She now believed she had known two separate people: Daredevil and Matt Murdock. Despite her own reservations, when Daredevil lost his way, Elektra returned to New York to help him, becoming his new "Stick" as she trained him to push himself forward to be a hero once more. It was a new role for the assassin, and a sign that she was walking a new, complex path.

Left: DAREDEVIL #13 (JAN. 2020)
Elektra returned to Daredevil's life, retraining the hero and later helping him steal billions of dollars from the Stormwyn family to redistribute to charities.

"I am Elektra, the assassin. To look upon me… is to see the end of life."

ELEKTRA

MUTANT MAESTROS

WOLVERINE

UNKILLABLE RONIN

Wolverine is one of the deadliest heroes in the world. He is a mutant with berserker rage, an unbreakable Adamantium skeleton and razor-sharp claws, quick healing ability, and exceptional fighting skills; a member of the X-Men, Avengers, and on occasion the Fantastic Four. But he's more than just a mutant hero. Logan—as he is known by his friends—is also a noble warrior, a modern-day samurai, with the training to match. Born James Howlett in the last years of the 19th century, Howlett's quick healing ability has given him a greatly extended life span—more than enough time to train with a number of martial arts masters and fight as part of several elite groups. Wolverine gained a love of Eastern philosophy in the early 20th century, and found it helped him keep the more bestial side of his nature in check.

A number of teachers—from Ogun to Bando Saboro to Professor Xavier—have made sure Wolverine's fighting skills complemented his mutant abilities. His success has also led others to try and recreate the process that made him so deadly. Romulus, one of Wolverine's many enemies, manipulated Wolverine's son Daken into hating his father and trained him to be a killer. Logan's clone Laura was also put through a grim and bloody training regime in an attempt to make her an even deadlier agent than her "father." Wolverine has stood firm against some of the most brutal killers in the world—including those who sacrificed their own humanity in search of deadlier abilities. From Lady Deathstrike, to the Hand and Sabretooth, it is Wolverine's training that has kept him alive for so long. He really is the best at what he does...

WOLVERINE #2 (MAY 2020) A killer mutant with berserker rage, Wolverine's long life has given him plenty of time to hone his deadly martial arts skills.

WOLVERINE #40 (MAY 2006) In the village of Jasmine Falls, Logan attempted to learn how to control his rage through the use of martial arts.

Code of Honor

Long before he joined the X-Men, Logan met Ogun, a martial arts master working for the Japanese military during the Japanese invasion of China. In due course, Ogun became Logan's first sensei.

While Logan had learned the art of assassination from the spy known as Seraph, Ogun introduced Logan to a new world of Eastern knowledge and skill. In the aftermath of World War II, Logan sought out another teacher, Bando Saburo, on Ogun's recommendation. Saburo taught the ex-ninja a better way of life in the small, picture-perfect Japanese village of Jasmine Falls. Logan enjoyed nearly five years of peace there. He trained with Saburo and fell in love with a woman called Itsu. The two were to have a child together until Itsu was murdered. While Logan didn't know it at the time, their unborn child survived and eventually took the name Daken. The boy would become a deadly warrior, raised by Romulus—one of Wolverine's many enemies—to have a deep hatred of his father.

Logan's martial arts training stayed strong and his love of Japan often brought him back to the country. When Professor Xavier enlisted him for a new X-Men team, his fellow mutants at first saw Wolverine as a wild man who loved beer and fighting. During a mission to Japan where they fought arms dealer Moses Magnum, Logan met one of his greatest loves: Mariko Yashida.

Mariko was from one of the noblest and most powerful families in Japan. The two fell instantly in love. Logan returned to New York, but when he thought Mariko was in danger, he traveled to Japan only to find out she had been married. Her father, Lord Shingen, long believed dead, had returned, aided by the Hand. He had married off his daughter to a Yakuza gangster to forge a stronger link with the Japanese underworld. When Logan went to check on Mariko, he learned her husband was beating her. Soon after, Logan was hit by a poisoned shuriken and brought before Lord Shingen. Shingen fought Logan and, with Logan still suffering from the poison in his system, easily defeated him, using only a wooden practice sword as he deemed Logan unworthy of a true blade.

"I'm the best at what I do. But what I do isn't very nice."

LOGAN

Above: WOLVERINE #2 (OCT. 1982)
After his defeat by Lord Shingen, Logan was aided by the lone assassin Yukio. The pair were soon attacked by the Hand, but Logan later learned it had been a ruse to make him trust Yukio.

Logan was helped to recover by Yukio, an assassin who seemed fixated by him. When Logan realized Shingen's rivals were planning to kill Mariko and her husband, he stopped them, but slipped into a berserker rage. Mariko had never seen that side of Logan and was horrified. It sent Logan into a spiral of self-loathing—one Yukio was willing to use to her advantage. When she accidentally killed Logan's old friend Asano Kimura, Wolverine began to realize he had been played. Yukio was working for Shingen. He set out to kill her, but couldn't bring himself to do it.

Having regained his sense of self-worth, Wolverine launched a one-man assault on Shingen's criminal empire, tearing apart in a matter of days what Shingen had spent years building. Logan used his skills to enter Shingen's home, dispatching the waiting Hand assassins. Mariko's husband, terrified, tried to flee with his wife and when confronted by Logan, threatened to kill her. Yukio came to their aid, killing the gangster. It placed Logan in Yukio's debt, and he let her go. He then faced Shingen. This time, the crime boss didn't use a practice blade. He was good, but Logan was better, and he killed the villain. Wolverine struggled to face Mariko after killing her father, but she declared he had saved the family honor; he was more worthy of the legendary blade than her father had ever been.

Sadly, Logan and Mariko's relationship ended in tragedy. The X-Men's old foe Mastermind manipulated Mariko into leaving Logan at the altar. While the villain's influence was later undone, Mariko was poisoned on the orders of Hand leader Matsu'o Tsurayaba. As the toxin took effect, Mariko begged Logan to end her life before the pain became too great. Wolverine complied, swearing vengeance on Matsu'o, whom he gruesomely punished every year on the anniversary of Mariko's death.

Like all great martial artists, Wolverine has also been a teacher. When a corrupted Ogun kidnapped Kitty Pryde, he trained her to be a killer. Logan helped free Kitty from Ogun's control, but had to kill his old master to save her. It was a telling moment for Logan. He went on to train Kitty and would later take charge of his own school of mutants. His first teacher had become a creature of evil, who killed without guilt. It showed Logan why he needed his code of honor.

In the following years, Wolverine often struggled to control his rage but, using the skills he had developed in the East, managed to do so. Those skills would also help him face enemies just as highly trained in martial arts as he was—but perhaps even deadlier.

Left and above right: WOLVERINE #4 (DEC. 1982) Lord Shingen wielded the honor sword of the Clan Yashida, forged 800 years before by the supreme swordsmith Masamune, but it was Wolverine's claws that landed the killing blow.

Below: WOLVERINE #57 (JUL. 1992) While trying to break her clan's links to organized crime, Mariko was poisoned with deadly blowfish toxin. Her last wish was for Logan to end her suffering.

Enemy Action

Wolverine has battled numerous skilled fighters —from the deadly assassins of the Hand, to the feral fury of Sabretooth. Some have been closely related to him, or connected to his origins.

One of the deadliest foes faced by Wolverine has been Lady Deathstrike. Yuriko Oyama was the daughter of Lord Dark Wind, a Japanese scientist and crimelord who originally invented the process that allowed Adamantium to be bonded with bone. While Yuriko was initially appalled by her father's criminal activities, she took over his work after his death, embraced her samurai roots, and sought to track down some Adamantium that Bullseye had stolen for use on his own skeleton. Searching with a special tracker, Yuriko instead came across Logan. A ferocious fight ensued, and Lady Deathstrike was defeated. It marked the start of a hatred that lasted long after her mortal body had died. To make herself deadlier, she visited Spiral's Body Shoppe and allowed the sorcerer to recreate her in a more menacing form that included Adamantium claws and bones.

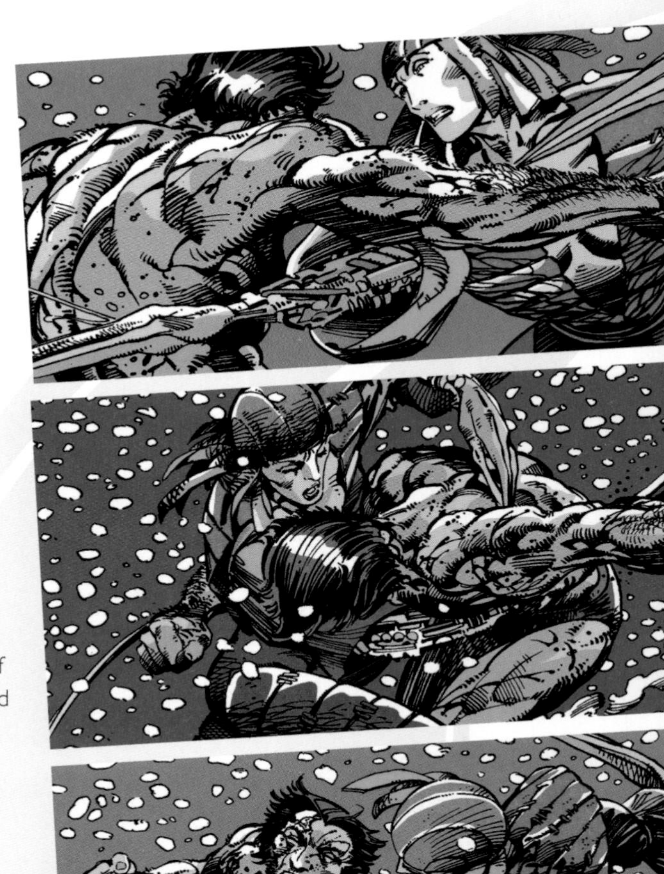

Along with three other cyborgs, Lady Deathstrike hunted Wolverine in a snowy New York, severely injuring him. As he healed, Logan reverted to an almost beast-like mental state. He survived with the help of young hero Katie Power. In a final showdown with Lady Deathstrike, Wolverine was stunned by the horrific changes Yuriko had undergone. Defeated, she begged for death, but he turned away. The two would fight again and again—at one point even being transported back to the time of the Spanish Civil War. Her hatred would cost Lady Deathstrike her life—but her essence lived on in digital form, and she later took over other bodies to renew her attack on the X-Men and Wolverine.

Surviving certain death seems to be a habit for many of Wolverine's foes. His first teacher, Ogun, survived the death of his body to possess others and renew his attack on his old student, while the Silver Samurai—the illegitimate son of Lord Shingen—confronted Wolverine in Hell long after his own death. Few have managed to inflict lasting damage on Wolverine, let alone kill him, but the mutant and Hand assassin named Gorgon came close.

Above and right: UNCANNY X-MEN #205 (MAY 1986)
Lady Deathstrike's cybernetic modifications, coupled with her martial arts skills, made her an extremely deadly—if tragic—enemy.

Gorgon was the head of the Dawn of the White Light—a death cult of mutants based in Japan—and he helped create an alliance between Hydra and the Hand. Having set a trap for Logan, Gorgon impaled Wolverine with his swords and used the Hand's arcane rites to resurrect him as one of its deadly assassins. The rest of Gorgon's plan was simple; Wolverine would kill other Super Heroes and the Hand would raise them from the dead to work alongside him. The brainwashed Wolverine tore his way through his fellow heroes, only his subconscious struggle against the Hand's programming keeping many of them alive. Northstar and others were killed before Captain America finally brought Logan in.

The event saw Logan battling the ninja assassin Elektra, who was working for spy agency S.H.I.E.L.D. She, too, was captured by Gorgon and reborn again as a Hand assassin. Wolverine was deprogrammed by S.H.I.E.L.D. and survived an assault on the agency's Helicarrier by the Hand's new super-powered assassins. Wolverine then went rogue to get revenge on the Hand, stealing three S.H.I.E.L.D.-modified Sentinels to help him obliterate the Hand assassins, before confronting their leaders. They summoned Elektra to fight him, but she was really in deep cover for S.H.I.E.L.D. to discover the group's endgame: an attack on the president. With help from Elektra, the Hand was finally torn apart.

WOLVERINE #29 (AUG. 2005) After breaking the Hand's control, Wolverine launched a ferocious one-man assault on the assassins—and was soon joined by Elektra.

"They're dead before they hit the ground!"

WOLVERINE

Left: WOLVERINE #31 (OCT. 2005) Logan faced Gorgon for a second time, stopping the mutant from killing Nick Fury. While Gorgon was the more skilled, Logan's anger gave him the edge.

However, Gorgon himself remained unsubdued. While Wolverine knew he was no match for the ninja's fighting skills, he had one trick to play. Gorgon was named for his mutant ability to turn people to stone with his gaze. When he tried it on Wolverine, Logan pulled up his claws so they reflected the power back at Gorgon. The villain turned himself to stone—and Wolverine shattered him.

One of Wolverine's toughest enemies shared his bloodline. His son Daken was raised in secret with the aim to destroy his father. Alongside his mutant abilities, he is a trained samurai and a master of several martial arts. He has proven to be more than a match for heroes and villains alike, and even adopted his father's name as part of Norman Osborn's Dark Avengers team. In recent times, and following his rebirth on the mutant paradise of Krakoa, Daken has finally bonded with Logan.

Left: WOLVERINE ORIGINS #13 (JUN. 2007) After years of hating his father, Daken eventually made peace with Wolverine and even joined a new incarnation of the X-Factor team, hoping to help out mutantkind.

Perhaps even deadlier than Daken is Wolverine's young female clone: Laura Kinney. Originally known only as X-23, Laura was created to kill and trained from birth to do so. Generated from cells taken from Logan and spliced with genetic material from Dr. Sarah Kinney—who became her birth mother—Laura was taught a range of martial arts and other deadly skills. Dr. Zander Rice, one of the project's heads, created a trigger scent that when used on a target would send Laura into a kill-frenzy. Her training was tough and without any semblance of warmth. The scientists behind the project even used the trigger scent on Dr. Sarah Kinney, forcing Laura to kill her own mother.

After escaping her creators, Laura eventually found her way to the X-Men and formed a bond with Wolverine, joining him on the deadly X-Force team. She has proven to be just as tough and skilled as Logan. She has also fought alongside Daken and saved her own clones, helping an innocent clone called Gabby accept her own abilities.

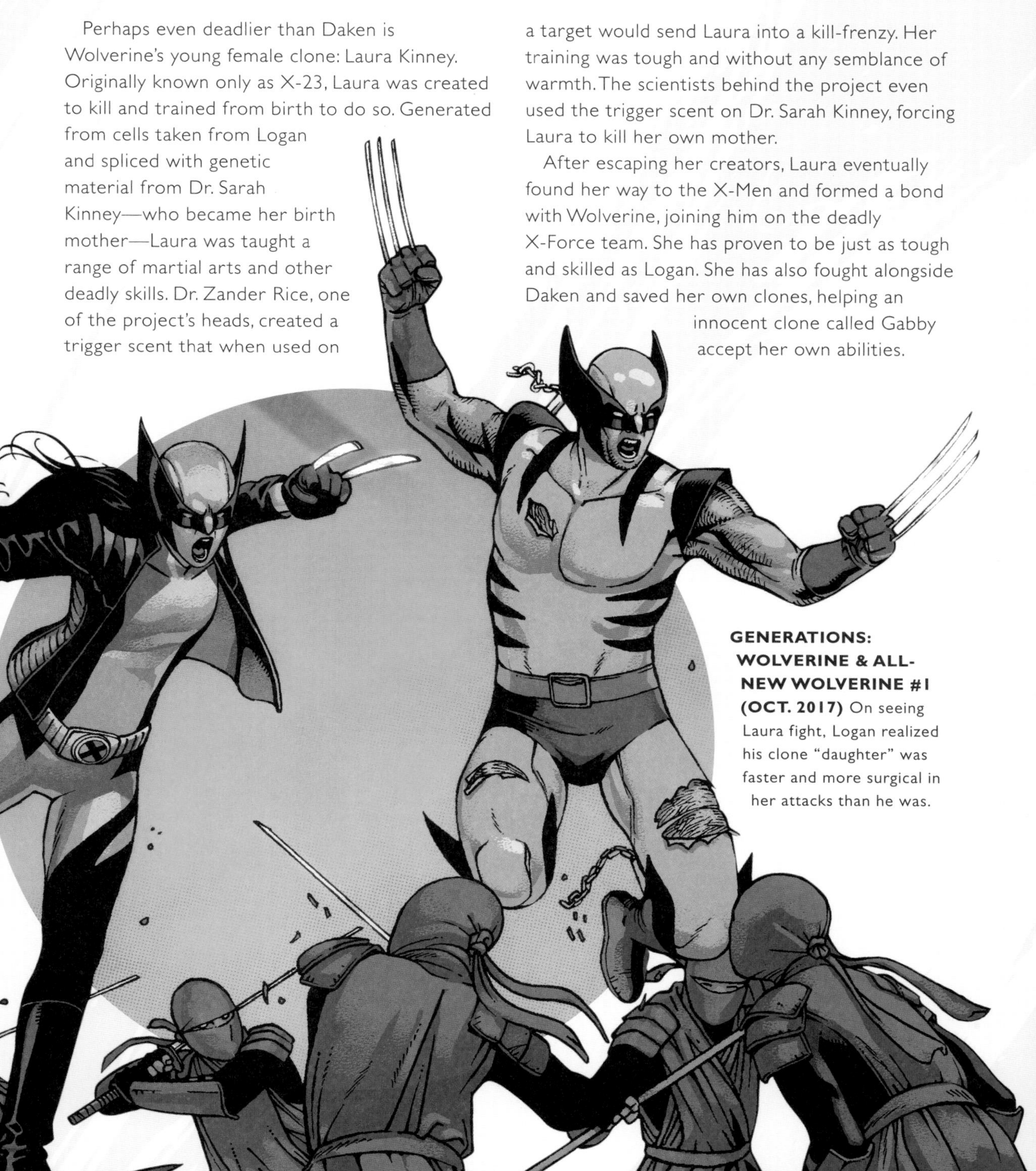

GENERATIONS: WOLVERINE & ALL-NEW WOLVERINE #1 (OCT. 2017) On seeing Laura fight, Logan realized his clone "daughter" was faster and more surgical in her attacks than he was.

There is one enemy who has plagued Logan since his early days: Victor Creed, aka Sabretooth. A berserker like Wolverine, but without any of Logan's morality, Creed is a serial killer, mercenary, and at one time an agent in the US government's clandestine Weapon X program—which saw subjects' super-powers harnessed for military purposes—alongside Logan. Both individuals received combat training while part of Weapon X, making them even deadlier fighters. While Logan is a killer, it is only ever as a last resort. Sabretooth has no such reservations. As well as being an archenemy of Iron Fist and Wolverine, one of his darkest feuds has been with Logan's teammate, Betsy Braddock, aka Psylocke—a hero whose martial arts prowess rivals that of Wolverine.

WOLVERINE: JAPAN'S MOST WANTED #1 (JUL. 2013) Sabretooth's feud with Wolverine stretched back over a century, and intensified when Sabretooth briefly became leader of the Hand.

"Even the Devil can bleed."

WOLVERINE

PSYLOCKE

THE PSIONIC NINJA

Psylocke combines ninja training with powerful psychic abilities. It marks her out as one of the X-Men's deadliest members and one of the world's greatest martial artists. She is also a hero with a troubled backstory, one who for many years was Elizabeth "Betsy" Braddock trapped in the body of Kwannon, an ex-Hand assassin. Now the two are separate entities again: two heroes with a shared and complicated past.

For much of her life, Betsy Braddock and her twin brother Brian thought they were just regular people. But then Brian was chosen by Merlyn to be the new Captain Britain and Betsy's psychic abilities kicked in. As Betsy also became a Super Hero, she learned her father, Jamie, had actually been born in the fantastical Arthurian realm of Otherworld and been sent to Earth by Merlyn with the explicit intent of creating a new Captain Britain. She learned her older brother, also called Jamie, was a powerful and dangerous mutant with the ability to bend reality itself with his mind. While a member of the X-Men, she fell foul of the multi-limbed cyborg, Spiral, and her Body Shoppe and was given a new Japanese form—one complete with exceptional martial arts skills. In time, she learned the body had formerly belonged to an assassin named Kwannon. For years Kwannon was dead, having died while inhabiting Betsy's old body. But when Betsy remade her own, original form, Kwannon also regained hers.

Now Betsy and Kwannon are living their own lives on the mutant island of Krakoa and are coming to terms with their new heroic identities: Betsy Braddock as Captain Britain, and Kwannon as Psylocke.

UNCANNY X-MEN #2 (MAR. 2016)

Two women have taken on the role of Psylocke—Betsy Braddock (pictured) and Kwannon. While the two had very different backgrounds, as Psylocke both used their psionic abilities to make their martial arts skills even deadlier.

Top: CAPTAIN BRITAIN #6 (JUN. 1985) When a Nazi version of Brian from another Earth attacked Betsy, he suffered the full impact of his psionic abilities as she defended herself.

Above: UNCANNY X-MEN #213 (JAN. 1987) New to the X-Men, Betsy held her own against Sabretooth when he infiltrated the X-Mansion, starting a feud that would last for years.

Mutant Martial Artist

Psylocke has proven to be one of the X-Men's deadliest martial artists. But the name—and at times body—has belonged to two very different people: Elizabeth "Betsy" Braddock, twin sister of Brian Braddock (aka Captain Britain) and Kwannon, a Japanese assassin.

Long before Betsy joined the X-Men, she worked for the British intelligence agency S.T.R.I.K.E.—specifically its psi-division. Her psionic abilities were already exceptionally strong—when she was attacked by a Nazi version of Captain Britain from a parallel world, her psychic powers fried his brain. Soon after, she briefly became Captain Britain herself, only to be blinded by the assassin Slaymaster. Betsy regained her vision when she was kidnapped by the interdimensional villain Mojo to star in one of his TV shows. *Wildways* was a big hit, and Betsy gained a new name: Psylocke.

Left: UNCANNY X-MEN #213 (JAN. 1987) Psylocke used Cerebro to boost her powers and aid her new X-Men allies, allowing her to quickly detect Sabretooth's incursion.

The New Mutants later rescued Betsy and she spent time at the X-Men's mansion, recovering from her ordeal. She fought Sabretooth when he infiltrated the property, heroically leading him away from casualties in the infirmary and holding her own against him until Wolverine could take over the fight. Her actions led to an invite to join the X-Men and also saw the start of a feud with Sabretooth.

When the X-Men were forced to take the Siege Perilous—an ancient mystical gateway that sent those who walked through it to new lives—Betsy washed up on an island in China and was found by Matsu'o Tsurayaba, a leader of the Hand. Using Spiral's Body Shoppe, Tsurayaba seemingly remade Betsy into an assassin. The new killer had both deadly martial arts skills and Betsy's psychic abilities. She could now create a psychic knife —the ultimate focus of her psychic powers—to injure or kill.

Taking the name Lady Mandarin, the new assassin started to work for Tsurayaba and the Mandarin as they launched a takeover of the Hong Kong underworld. The Hand took over crimelord Emil Vachon's old base, and there Tsurayaba helped train his new killer, before sending her after a weakened Wolverine. Lady Mandarin defeated Logan and began using her psychic skills to turn him into an assassin for the Hand. When she used her psychic knife on Logan, however, it triggered her own memories, and with the help of Wolverine, Betsy remembered who she really was.

Left: UNCANNY X-MEN #256 (DEC. 1989) Remade by the Body Shoppe, Betsy briefly took the name Lady Mandarin and became a deadly enforcer for her namesake.

JUBILEE'S FIREWORKS TOOK OUT THE YACHT'S ENGINES AN' INTERNAL POWER.
GUARDS ARE UP TO US.
PARDON MY ASKING, O FEARLESS LEADER...
...BUT THIS IS SUPPOSED TO BE A PROBLEM?

UNCANNY X-MEN #268 (SEP. 1990) Psylocke was still finding her place in the X-Men when she helped Wolverine and Black Widow fight the Hand and agents of Hydra in Madripoor.

Psylocke joined forces with Wolverine and firework-conjuring mutant Jubilee to defeat the Mandarin. She was not sure if the X-Men would accept her in her new form, or if she could even trust herself. In time, though, she became one of the X-Men's most powerful members, helping them against the likes of Magneto and the Shadow King. But her world was shaken to its core when a woman appeared in the X-Mansion claiming to be the real Betsy Braddock. Psylocke eventually learned the truth about her strange transformation: her new body was that of Tsurayaba's lover, a ninja called Kwannon.

Kwannon had been raised by the Hand to be one of its assassins. When she fell in love and had a child, the Hand killed her lover and took the child away from her. Kwannon went on to become the main assassin for a Japanese crimelord named Lord Nyoirin, and the lover of Matsu'o Tsurayaba. When the Hand and Lord Nyoirin went to war with each other, Kwannon found herself honor-bound to fight her lover, but she fell from a cliff and was left comatose.

Soon after, Spiral used her powers to change Betsy into her new form and used Kwannon's body to do so. It turned out Spiral had gone even further, merging both personas and splitting their abilities and souls. Kwannon lived, as did Betsy, and both shared part of the other's skills and soul, but Kwannon now had Betsy's body and vice versa.

Calling herself Revanche, Kwannon remained with the X-Men for a brief period before falling victim to the pernicious Legacy Virus. Kwannon returned home and asked Tsurayaba to end her suffering. He complied, and as Kwannon died, she returned the parts of her own consciousness that had once been Betsy's. Psylocke regained all her old powers and abilities and felt complete again. She was still in Kwannon's body, but was now content. The combination of Kwannon's training as a ninja and assassin combined with Betsy's exceptional psychic powers made her a key member of the X-Men, and one whose deadly abilities rivaled those of Wolverine. But it wasn't the end of the story for both women.

X-MEN #32 (MAY 1994) Spiral's changes linked Betsy and Kwannon together body and soul. Needless to say, Psylocke was not happy with Spiral's actions.

Psylocke Returns

Psylocke soon became a mainstay of the X-Men, although her time with them was often brutal and she was killed more than once.

Her feud with Sabretooth took a deadly turn when he escaped confinement at the X-Mansion. Psylocke tried to protect teammate Meltdown and seemed to get the better of Sabretooth by using her psychic knife on him—only to find it no longer had an impact on Sabretooth's mind. The villain escaped, but not before slashing Betsy, leaving her close to death. Archangel and Wolverine found a way to save her life using the mystical force of the Crimson Dawn, a life-giving potion from the realm of the same name. The process changed Psylocke again, giving her greater powers and a strange marking over her left eye.

Psylocke's connection to the Crimson Dawn led to its leader, Proctor Kuragari, taking her and trying to transform her into his deadly bride. She escaped with the help of Archangel and Wolverine.

Betsy was killed fighting the mutant villain Vargas, only to be resurrected by her brother Jamie Braddock a year later. He increased his sister's powers so she could later help defeat an ancient cosmic entity known as the First Fallen. She was also selected by Merlyn's daughter, Roma, to join the Exiles: a pan-dimensional team of heroes.

While fighting alongside the Exiles, Psylocke confronted an alternate version of Slaymaster, who was visiting Earths and killing various versions of Betsy Braddock. Still suffering from her original confrontation with her own Earth's Slaymaster, Psylocke wasn't sure she could defeat him. She was helped by an alternate incarnation of Ogun, Wolverine's old sensei, who trained Betsy so she could take her revenge—and help Ogun achieve his own, because in his world, Slaymaster had killed his student, Lady Mandarin. With Ogun's extra training, Psylocke was more than a match for Slaymaster and ended his reign of terror.

Having left the Exiles, Betsy was tricked into traveling to Japan to confront Matsu'o Tsurayaba. Wolverine had been true to his word after Tsurayaba caused the death of his beloved Mariko and had been removing a piece of Tsurayaba's body every year, leaving him horribly disfigured and seeking death. Psylocke fought Wolverine to try to stop him continuing his vendetta, and then used her own abilities to fulfill Tsurayaba's wish to die. As she killed him, Betsy used her psychic abilities to give him one last vision of his beloved Kwannon.

HUNT FOR WOLVERINE: MYSTERY IN MADRIPOOR #1 (JUL. 2018) Wolverine helped Psylocke hone her deadly abilities and adapt to her new form.

"At last I am myself!"

BETSY BRADDOCK

Psylocke, along with the X-Men, grieved when Wolverine seemingly died encased in Adamantium, but when his body went missing, she joined the search for him. Psylocke traveled to Madripoor and came into conflict with a psychic vampire called Sapphire Styx. Styx consumed her soul, but Betsy managed to stay alive inside the creature's mind—eventually defeating her and recreating her own, original body with the power of the souls Styx had previously consumed. Betsy once more looked like her original self, while at the same time, Kwannon was reborn in her own body, confused and angry.

While Betsy remained with the X-Men, Kwannon's path also led to the team. She killed Joseph—a clone of Magneto—to stop him wiping out mutantkind, and then tried to come to terms with her return. Following the creation of the mutant safe haven Krakoa, both Betsy and Kwannon moved there, but tried to avoid each other.

Kwannon took the name Psylocke and joined mutant clone X-23 and Cable to investigate a powerful mutant threat that had plagued her meditation, while Betsy was drawn to the pocket dimension of Otherworld. Following her brother Brian's defeat by Morgan Le Fey, she became the new Captain Britain. Finally, Kwannon and Betsy had found a peace, of sorts, as X-Men and heroes.

Top left: HUNT FOR WOLVERINE: MYSTERY IN MADRIPOOR #4 (OCT. 2018) Betsy's soul was consumed by Sapphire Styx. When she escaped and remade herself, she returned to her original appearance.

Left: FALLEN ANGELS #6 (MAR. 2020) Still getting used to being alive again, Kwannon used her psionic powers in new ways—such as giving herself the power of flight.

"This challenge is to the death, remember? So how about we see just how good you really are?"

PSYLOCKE

SPIES AND MERCENARIES

SPIES AND MERCENARIES

KILL AND BE KILLED

Perhaps the most dangerous enemies of all are those who hire themselves out to the highest bidder and lurk in the shadows ready to strike. Some of these martial artists consider themselves heroes and others relish their role as killers for hire. Some have been trained by their governments and sent out into the world to cause mayhem, while others have mysterious backgrounds that even they have forgotten. In this murky world of black ops, international espionage, and ruthless assassins there is a lot of competition between fighters and mercy is in short supply.

Black Widow was a trained Soviet spy, sent to the West to bring chaos and steal files from Tony Stark. In time she found a better life in the States, choosing to turn her back on her unsavory past and instead trying to use her deadly skills as a force for good, either working solo or fighting alongside S.H.I.E.L.D. and the Avengers. Some heroes have taken on the role of Ronin, wanting to work covertly and unrecognized while using their amazing fighting skills to make the world a better place.

Then there are the cold-blooded killers—among them Batroc, Taskmaster, Deadpool, and Bullseye—mercenaries who have killed for both money and entertainment. Some, such as Deadpool and Batroc, have their own moral codes while others, like Bullseye, revel in the death they bring. All of these spies, renegade heroes, and villains share one thing in common—they have martial arts skills few can match.

TASKMASTER #1 (NOV. 2020) Taskmaster is both a ruthless killer and a tragic figure. A S.H.I.E.L.D. agent who went deep undercover, his ability to mimic any move came at a price—the wiping of his past memories.

BLACK WIDOW: DEADLY ORIGIN #1 (JAN. 2010) Natasha thought of Logan as her "little uncle" and disobeyed an order to assassinate him.

Black Widow: Trained to Kill

Natalia Romanova was born in Stalingrad, USSR, in 1928. Shortly after her birth, Natalia (usually known as Natasha) was saved from a burning building by Soviet soldier Ivan Petrovitch. Ivan adopted her as his own daughter.

While Ivan went to war, Natasha was selected to be part of the Red Room, a specialist operation that brought together orphaned girls to be trained as spies and assassins. By the start of World War II, Natasha was a student of Russian spy Taras Romanov and was receiving martial arts training from the hired assassin Logan (later known as Wolverine). She learned countless techniques for assassination and, as her graduation test, was ordered to kill Logan—despite the bond they had formed. Instead, she let him escape, after learning Logan had only been there to assassinate Taras.

It was a bond that came to her rescue when Natasha was kidnapped by the Hand. The ninja cult recognized her potential and planned to turn her into one of its master assassins. Her strong will helped her resist the Hand's brainwashing techniques, and she was rescued by Logan and Captain America. Returning to Russia, her combat training intensified, and Natasha was given false memories to cover up the programming—instilling in her memories of a ballet career. Her martial arts training included karate, savate, jujitsu, and boxing, and she proved to be the Red Room's top student.

Natasha was soon sent out into the world on missions to assassinate targets. She also met Bucky Barnes, Captain America's World War II sidekick, who had himself been captured by the Soviets and reprogrammed as the Winter Soldier. The two trained together and had a brief relationship. Natasha later married Soviet hero Alexei Shostakov. When he was selected to be the Red Guardian (the Soviet Union's answer to Captain America), the authorities faked his death. It was many years before Natasha learned the truth.

Natasha became a Russian agent serving in the West and was sent to the US to kill billionaire inventor Tony Stark and Russian defector Anton Vanko. While her mission failed, she later seduced Stark to steal technology from his company. Natasha remained a Russian asset until she partnered with the hero Hawkeye. While at first she sought to use the archer to further her missions in the West, his idealism changed her, and she severed contact with her Soviet handlers.

Brought into S.H.I.E.L.D. as one of its operatives, Natasha fought alongside the Avengers, starting a long connection with the team. Basing herself in New York, she created a new look—one more fitting to her new life. She donned a leather catsuit while fighting, and used a "Widow's line" to swing between buildings. Natasha also teamed up with Daredevil, the two becoming an effective crime-fighting unit. Although the pair eventually split, they remained close friends. Years later, when Natasha was poisoned, it was Daredevil she turned to. In return, she helped him fight the Hand with Stone of the Chaste when the clan tried to resurrect Matt's ex-love, Elektra.

UNCANNY X-MEN #268 (SEP. 1990) In 1941, the Hand wanted to mold a young Natasha into one of their own, having heard about her natural aptitude for martial arts.

BLACK WIDOW: DEADLY ORIGIN #3 (MAR. 2010) Natasha had an intense relationship with Matt Murdock, especially when they moved to San Francisco and continued to fight crime together.

Above: BLACK WIDOW #1 (JUN. 1999)
Natasha helped free her successor, Yelena, from the Black Widow program. Following Natasha's death, Yelena adopted the identity once again and started to use her skills as a force for good.

As well as occasionally fighting as an Avenger, Natasha formed a short-lived team called the Champions, alongside heroes Hercules, Angel, Iceman, and Ghost Rider. Based in Los Angeles, the team found themselves fighting a number of dangerous foes, including a group of Russian super-powered agents.

Natasha's defection to the West didn't signify the end of the Black Widow program back home. The training of the other women continued. The most promising operative was Yelena Belova, who claimed the name Black Widow and pitted herself against Natasha.

Left: SECRET EMPIRE #7 (SEP. 2017) Natasha originally planned to assassinate the Hydra Captain America, but instead prevented Spider-Man (Miles Morales) from becoming a murderer.

Above: SECRET EMPIRE #7 (SEP. 2017) Saving Miles Morales from taking a dark path came at great cost for Natasha—the evil Captain America broke her neck with his shield, killing her.

However, Natasha eventually helped Yelena break free from her handlers. Natasha's life as a spy also led to her facing some of the deadliest assassins in the world, including Elektra.

When an evil version of Steve Rogers gained a Cosmic Cube and used it to cause a Hydra takeover of the US, Natasha joined the Underground—a group assembled to fight the country's new fascist rulers. Increasingly annoyed at the Underground's tactics, she set off alone to assassinate Steve Rogers. A new incarnation of the Champions went along with her. Spider-Man Miles Morales ended up confronting Captain America, but when Black Widow intervened, she was hit and killed by Cap's shield. When the real Steve Rogers returned and defeated his evil doppelgänger, Hydra was overthrown, but Natasha, among other heroes, remained dead.

Above: WEB OF BLACK WIDOW #1 (NOV. 2019)
Natasha's strength and endurance were boosted by an experimental Soviet serum. It also granted her increased longevity and rapid healing.

Opposite: WEB OF BLACK WIDOW #2 (DEC. 2019)
Reborn as a clone, Natasha was haunted by her past, with some of her memories fragmented and missing.

Yelena took on the role of the Black Widow once again, until she learned that Natasha was back. The original Black Widow had been cloned by the Red Room and imprinted with her old memories. Playing along with the institution's mind games, Natasha learned the Red Room had cloned all its best operatives, so she used her deadly skills to destroy it once and for all. Natasha was still plagued by memories of those she had killed while working for the Red Room and decided to make amends by hunting down the people who had ordered or benefited from her past actions. At the same time, she started to suffer memory loss—just as someone who looked like the Black Widow was seen killing innocent people. It turned out that another agent of the Red Room—Anya—had been behind the deaths.

Right: WEB OF BLACK WIDOW #5 (MAR. 2020) While a solo operator, Natasha knew when to call in allies for help—especially when she planned to build a web to capture a killer.

Anya had trained alongside Natasha and had then tried to create a new generation of assassins. Natasha managed to end those plans and rescue the young, would-be killers, but Anya returned seeking revenge. Natasha decided to lay a trap for her—one that relied on her allies Yelena, Iron Man, Bucky, Hawkeye, and Captain America. Her friends made it look like they had fallen for Anya's deception, allowing Natasha to build her own web to bring her enemy out into the open and capture her. With Anya in custody, Tony Stark helped Natasha with her memory problems, making her whole again and able to remember all her past actions—the good and the bad.

Right: NEW AVENGERS #11 (NOV. 2005) As the first Ronin, Maya Lopez found that even her martial arts skills couldn't defeat overwhelming odds.

Below: NEW AVENGERS #12 (DEC. 2005) When Daredevil was forced to turn down Captain America's request for help, he suggested Maya Lopez, knowing her skills rivaled his own.

Ronin: Heroes in Disguise

Ronin is a Japanese term for a wandering, masterless samurai. The name has been taken by several heroes when they felt their normal heroic identity could no longer be used.

While each "Ronin" has been very different, they all share one important trait: exceptional fighting skills. The first was Maya Lopez. Born deaf, Maya has photographic reflexes—she can copy any move she sees. Her mobster father was killed by Wilson Fisk, but before his death he asked the Kingpin to raise his daughter. Fisk did just that, sending her to the best schools. She became a highly trained martial artist and her photographic reflexes helped her fight like Daredevil, Bullseye, and members of the Hand. Fisk tried to use Maya in a plot to destroy Daredevil, having raised her to have a burning hatred of the hero. When they first fought, Maya defeated Daredevil, only to learn the Kingpin had lied to her. In revenge, she shot Fisk in the face, blinding him.

As well as adopting the name Echo, Maya took on the Ronin identity to make a new start. She joined the Avengers after Daredevil recommended her to Captain America. When the team went to Japan, Ronin was sent to infiltrate the base of the Clan Yashida (once home to Wolverine's dead love, Mariko) where she witnessed a meeting between ninja cult the Hand, terrorist organization Hydra, and the Silver Samurai, who had taken over as leader of the Clan Yashida. Ronin was spotted by the Hand and forced to fight her way free to warn the Avengers. Despite the overwhelming numbers against them, the Avengers managed to arrest Madame Hydra. Ronin decided to remain in Japan to investigate the Hand's new leader, Elektra.

When Maya's Ronin costume was delivered to Iron Fist with a note, the Avengers knew she was in trouble—or dead. Clint Barton had recently met with his old Avengers teammates and wanted to help, but felt he could no longer use Hawkeye as an identity. Instead, he took on the role of Ronin and traveled to Japan with the Avengers to find out what had happened to Maya. What the Avengers did not know was that Maya had already been killed by the Hand and resurrected as one of its deadly agents. Luckily Doctor Strange was able to break the Hand's hold over her. Back in control, Maya gained her revenge and killed Elektra, only to learn that she had not been the real Elektra, but a Skrull agent

NEW AVENGERS #27 (APR. 2007) While seeking information about the Hand's new leader, Maya found herself outnumbered by the assassins and was killed by Elektra.

"If you're reading this, I'm probably dead."

MAYA LOPEZ

Following her rescue, Maya thought it was only fitting that Clint continued in the role of Ronin. Clint's time as Ronin was a troubled one—not just for Clint, but for many heroes in the US. He fought against the Skrulls, helping stop their attempted invasion of Earth, but when devious industrialist Norman Osborn replaced the spy agency S.H.I.E.L.D. with H.A.M.M.E.R. and created his own Avengers, Clint found himself an outlaw. He could only watch as Osborn introduced the world to a new Avengers team—one that included the villain Bullseye in the guise of Hawkeye.

Clint decided that the only way to end Norman Osborn's Dark Reign was to kill him. He managed to infiltrate the HQ of Osborn's Avengers and take out a number of the team, including Bullseye, before confronting Osborn himself.

However, Osborn had a personal protection shield that stopped Ronin's bullets hitting home. Ares—another of Osborn's Avengers—intervened and defeated Ronin, but Mockingbird joined forces with some heroic female friends to rescue him. Ronin then took part in the final fight against Osborn when the villain launched a full-scale assault on Asgard. In the aftermath, Clint resumed his Hawkeye identity.

Clint later found himself fighting a new incarnation of Ronin when ex-Red Guardian Alexei Shostakov used the role in an attempt to restore the glory of the old Soviet Union. He was defeated by Black Widow, Hawkeye, and Mockingbird, but was later found to have been a Life Model Decoy (a highly lifelike android sometimes used by S.H.I.E.L.D.).

Left: NEW AVENGERS ANNUAL #2 (FEB. 2008)
Clint Barton took on the role of Ronin following his return from the dead, having been both killed and resurrected by the Scarlet Witch's magic.

Opposite left: DARK REIGN: THE LIST—AVENGERS #1 (NOV. 2009) Clint, as Ronin, infiltrated Osborn's base and ruthlessly took out most of his Avengers' team, including Bullseye.

The Ronin identity lay dormant for some time. When the Mad Titan Thanos' emissaries launched an attack on Earth, street hero Luke Cage and his allies fought to stop them. An unnamed hero—at first, dressed in a makeshift Halloween Spider-Man costume to protect his identity—fought alongside them. The hero turned out to be Blade, the vampire slayer, and he joined Luke Cage's new Avengers as the fourth incarnation of Ronin—having found the Ronin outfit in a bag of Hawkeye's old stuff. As part of his war on vampires—and his own extended lifespan—Blade had been highly trained in various martial arts. The Avengers helped him end the threat of black magic cult the Deathwalkers.

When Clint took on the Hood's criminal empire, Bullseye was hired to use the Ronin identity to ruin Clint's reputation. It nearly worked, but Clint eventually tracked down Bullseye and, dressed as Bullseye himself, defeated him—leaving Bullseye in his Ronin costume pinned down by arrows for the authorities to deal with. It is only a matter of time before another hero takes on the mantle of Ronin.

Right: MIGHTY AVENGERS #4 (FEB. 2014) While Blade was concealing his true identity from an evil cult, he still wore his leather jacket over the Ronin costume.

DAREDEVIL: END OF DAYS #4 (MAR. 2013) In one potential future, Bullseye killed Daredevil and then committed suicide.

"Haven't you heard? I'm a cold-blooded killer."

BULLSEYE

Not all the greatest martial artists are heroes—many have chosen to sell their skills to the highest bidder. Bullseye, Taskmaster, Batroc, and Deadpool are among the most dangerous and unpredictable of them all.

Bullseye's past is filled with lies and fake personal histories; several have him working for the National Security Agency as an assassin before going freelance. Psychotic from an early age, Bullseye—who has used the names Lester and Benjamin in some stories—once claimed that he gained the nickname "Bullseye" after killing a batter with a pitch in a baseball match. While Bullseye is most connected with villainous types, he technically went legitimate during Norman Osborn's time in charge of national security, taking on the role of Hawkeye in Norman Osborn's Dark Avengers after a stint in the government-sanctioned Thunderbolts.

As well as his military training and martial arts skills, Bullseye's deadliest ability is that he can make anything a deadly weapon, as he never misses a target. Over the years, Bullseye has killed people with playing cards, pens, and even one of his own teeth. One hero in particular has been a target for the killer: Daredevil. Bullseye originally lured Daredevil to a circus—hoping to defeat him in front of the media and make a name for himself. While at first he got the better of Daredevil, the hero soon recovered and brought Bullseye to justice, heralding the start of Bullseye's obsessive hatred of the Man Without Fear. He has inflicted more damage on Daredevil than any of Matt's other enemies, having killed two of his great loves: Elektra and Karen Page. He also tried to kill Matt's wife, Milla Donovan.

It seems impossible to stop Bullseye for good. Over the years, he's come back from a brain tumor, paralysis, and even death at the hands of Daredevil. No matter what has happened to him, he has always returned even deadlier—with Daredevil usually in his sights.

DAREDEVIL #169 (MAR. 1981) A brain tumor started to give Bullseye hallucinations that Daredevil was everywhere he looked.

Another villain who worked with Osborn during his "Dark Reign" was Tony Masters, aka Taskmaster. The mercenary was put in charge of the Camp Hammond training facility in Stamford where Tony Stark had started to train Super Heroes before Osborn's rise. Captain America has called Taskmaster one of the deadliest people on Earth and the killer has gone head-to-head with all the best fighters in the world. Thanks to his photographic reflexes—an ability to perfectly copy the moves of anyone he encounters—Taskmaster has continuously increased his skills.

TASKMASTER #2 (DEC. 2010) When a bounty was put out on him, Taskmaster found himself attacked by agents working for Hydra.

CAPTAIN AMERICA #45 (FEB. 2009) A powerful kick from Batroc the Leaper was enough to send Bucky Barnes flying during Barnes' time as Captain America.

He has also taught a number of villains and henchmen at his specialist school and trained John Walker (the future US Agent) to take over the role of Captain America.

Taskmaster is also a villain with tragic origins—he was once a heroic S.H.I.E.L.D. agent, but can no longer remember his own past. While he was with S.H.I.E.L.D., Masters gained powers similar to that of Captain America when a dying scientist injected him with the Nazi version of the Super-Soldier serum. It increased his skills, but his ability to remember movements overwrote his established memories. Tony eventually started to forget his own past—even his own family and fellow S.H.I.E.L.D. agents—and started to become a villain. His wife became his handler for S.H.I.E.L.D. under the cover of getting him criminal jobs. Taskmaster has occasionally recovered his memory, and at one point even joined Captain America's covert Avengers team, but he soon slipped back into his old ways.

Georges Batroc has never been an Avenger, but he has faced off against Captain America a number of times. He was born in France and was originally a member of the French Foreign Legion before deciding to sell his skills to the highest bidder. He is a master of savate and has knowledge of a number of other martial arts. He is also amazingly skilled at parkour, hence his dynamic fighting style that has produced his nickname: "Batroc the Leaper." While he might not have the super-powers of other high-ranking mercenaries, Batroc's amazing skill makes up for it. He's even led his own team of mercenaries, dubbed "Batroc's Battalion."

DEADPOOL: ASSASSIN #1 (AUG. 2018)
Deadpool's quick-talking humor often distracts from his exceptional fighting skills. Even an army of ninjas was unable to stop him... or shut him up.

Among all of the mercenaries in the world, however, they don't come much more bizarre than the "Merc with a Mouth," Deadpool. Wade Wilson was born in Canada and joined the US Special Forces, but was kicked out for refusing to obey orders. Wade had fallen in love with a woman named Vanessa Carlysle when he found out he had terminal cancer. He ended up in Department K, which had worked with Department X on the mutant Wolverine. Wade's cancer was briefly halted when he was given implants derived from Wolverine's healing factor. When the cancer returned, he was transferred to the Hospice, a facility that supposedly treated superhumans with serious illnesses. In reality, they were test subjects for the facility's head, Doctor Killebrew, to experiment on. Wade heard the staff use the term "Deadpool" as they bet on who would be the next "patient" to die. When Wade's enhanced healing ability kicked back in, he managed to escape, and soon became a gun for hire.

Since Wade first went freelance, he has fought with some of the toughest and meanest entities in existence. He is trained in a variety of martial arts and has held his own against the best fighters in the world—his unpredictability making him even deadlier. He has formed his own group of killers for hire called Mercs for Money and fought alongside mutants such as Wolverine and Psylocke in the X-Force. While he can be a great ally in a tight situation, he can also be highly dangerous. As far as Deadpool is concerned, with great power comes no responsibility.

"What a *weird* day. I'm having fun, and I haven't killed anybody."

DEADPOOL

“SPACE FU”

"SPACE FU"

INTERSTELLAR MARTIAL ARTS

Beyond the Earth, alien races have developed their own specialist fighting techniques. Some, such as the shape-changing Skrulls, use science to grant select members super-powers, while others, such as the avian-like Shi'ar, naturally gain fantastical abilities—the elite becoming part of the Imperial Guard. Several galactic civilizations have created styles of martial arts unique to them. The Skrulls' ancient enemies, the Kree, have had a long tradition of forming their own fighting styles, while offshoots of their race—such as the exiled Priests of Pama—developed skills to protect themselves as they sought out the so-called Celestial Madonna, taking their expertise to Earth and other worlds.

The Inhumans, who were originally created by the Kree, settled on Earth and established their own religion and beliefs—including a very effective fighting style best exemplified by the warrior known as Karnak. Thanos, one of the most powerful beings in the universe, made sure his adopted daughter, Gamora, had the best teachers in the cosmos as she honed her martial arts skills to a fine sword-point. Of course, there is not just life on alien planets—there are also parallel Earths spread out through reality and from one such Earth hailed a very strange hero: a maelstrom of feathered fury called Howard. From Gamora, the deadliest woman in the galaxy, to Howard the Duck, master of "quak fu," some heroes have become experts at their own styles of martial arts, styles perhaps best described as "space fu."

KARNAK #3 (JUN. 2016) Karnak is not only an exceptional martial artist, his training gives him the ability to find the weak point in any object or enemy.

GUARDIANS OF THE GALAXY #4 (AUG. 2013) The last survivor of her race, Gamora was raised by Thanos to be the ultimate warrior before she realized his true nature.

Gamora: Deadliest Woman in the Galaxy

Raised by the Mad Titan Thanos to be the ultimate assassin, Gamora found her true home with the Guardians of the Galaxy.

When Thanos faced the Magus, an enemy who knew his every move, he traveled to the future seeking someone he could turn into a weapon to use against him. Thanos saved a young girl named Gamora when her homeworld and the people who lived there—the peace-loving Zen Whoberis—were wiped out by Magus' Church of Universal Truth. He brought her back to his own time and trained her to be the deadliest woman in the galaxy. Thanos raised Gamora alongside Nebula—a part-humanoid, part-cyborg being who believed Thanos was her grandfather—but Nebula was never quite as effective as her "sister" and the two often came to blows as Nebula would try, and fail, to prove herself the superior fighter.

When Thanos' spaceship home, *Sanctuary II*, visited Tartoonla #7, a teenage Gamora ventured out alone—only to be attacked and almost killed by thugs. Thanos rescued her and used advanced technology to upgrade Gamora's physical form—making her even stronger, faster, and tougher. Gamora was trained in all the fighting arts known to Thanos, excelling in them all. She also became a master tactician and weapons expert—though she always preferred to use bladed weapons.

Although Gamora failed to assassinate the Magus, she eventually helped Adam Warlock—created to be the perfect future human—defeat him. Along the way, she started to reflect on her own bloody past and turned on Thanos when she realized his true goal was to use the Infinity Stones to destroy the galaxy. Thanos killed his adopted daughter, but Gamora found herself still sentient and living in one of the Infinity Stones—the Soul Stone—with Adam Warlock and Pip the Troll, finding peace there for a short time.

When Thanos used the Infinity Gauntlet to control all the Infinity Stones—including the Soul Stone—Warlock, Gamora, and Pip emerged to join the fight against him. In the aftermath of Thanos' defeat, Warlock formed the Infinity Watch, with Gamora working alongside him to protect the galaxy. In time, the team separated and Gamora formed the Graces, becoming

GAMORA #1 (FEB. 2017)
A highly skilled fighter herself, Nebula was always jealous of her older "sister's" greater fighting skills during their sparring sessions.

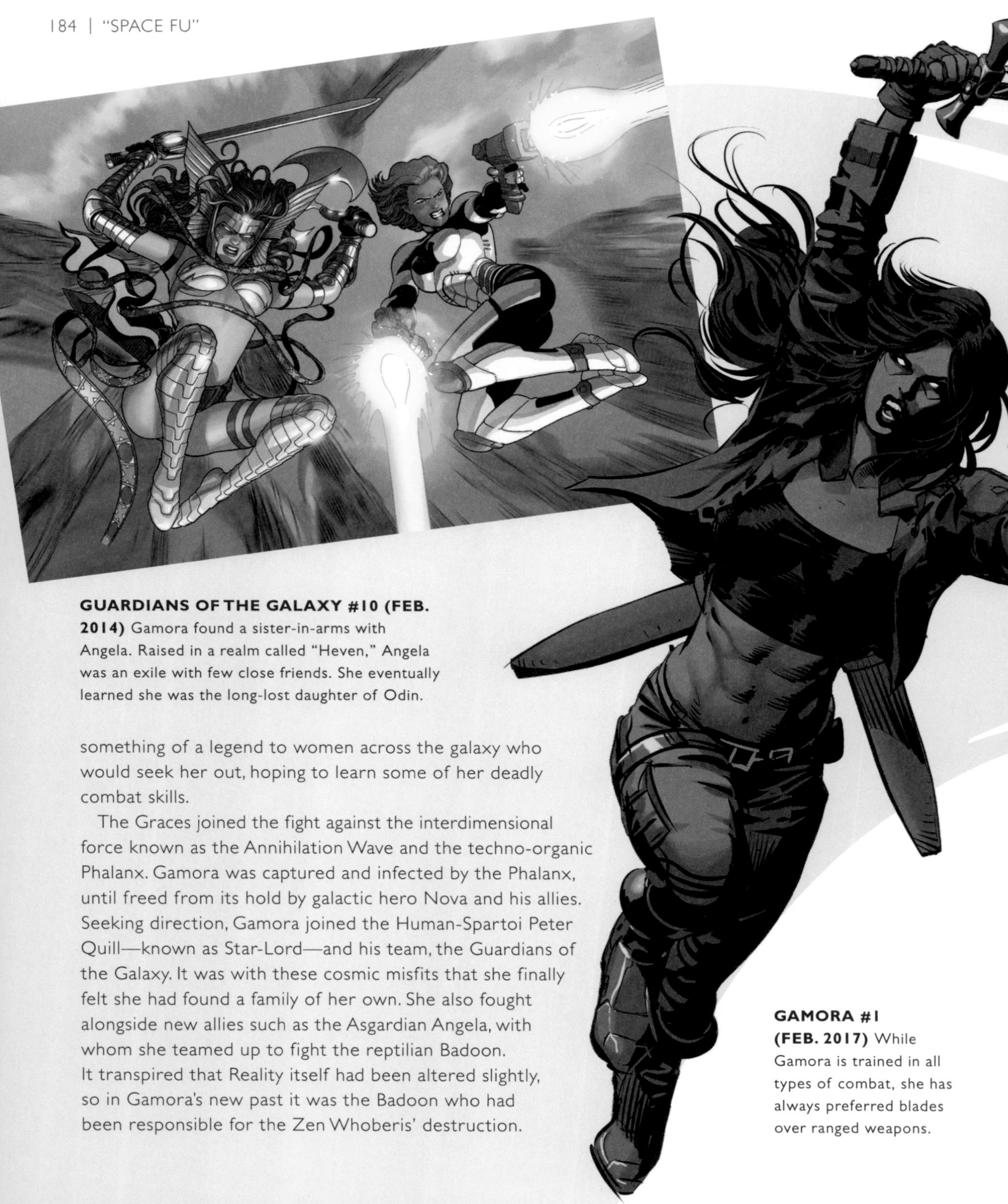

GUARDIANS OF THE GALAXY #10 (FEB. 2014) Gamora found a sister-in-arms with Angela. Raised in a realm called "Heven," Angela was an exile with few close friends. She eventually learned she was the long-lost daughter of Odin.

something of a legend to women across the galaxy who would seek her out, hoping to learn some of her deadly combat skills.

The Graces joined the fight against the interdimensional force known as the Annihilation Wave and the techno-organic Phalanx. Gamora was captured and infected by the Phalanx, until freed from its hold by galactic hero Nova and his allies. Seeking direction, Gamora joined the Human-Spartoi Peter Quill—known as Star-Lord—and his team, the Guardians of the Galaxy. It was with these cosmic misfits that she finally felt she had found a family of her own. She also fought alongside new allies such as the Asgardian Angela, with whom she teamed up to fight the reptilian Badoon. It transpired that Reality itself had been altered slightly, so in Gamora's new past it was the Badoon who had been responsible for the Zen Whoberis' destruction.

GAMORA #1 (FEB. 2017) While Gamora is trained in all types of combat, she has always preferred blades over ranged weapons.

INFINITY WARS PRIME #1 (SEP. 2018) After years of wanting her "father" dead, Gamora finally killed him using a sword that had the Power Stone built into it.

When Gamora found herself haunted by an older version of herself, she realized a portion of her essence had remained trapped in the Soul Stone years before and she struck out alone to find the stone. Gamora forced a dwarf of Nidavellir to create armor and a sword for her—the Infinity Blade—and placed the Power Stone into the weapon. She then went in search of her ultimate enemy: Thanos. As she killed her "father," Thanos warned Gamora that he would return and she would be his requiem.

Gamora took Requiem as her new name and began hunting the rest of the Infinity Stones, eventually managing to free her trapped essence from the Soul Stone. That stone harbored a dark secret: Devondra, a creature that fed off souls sent there. To buy herself time to deal with the creature, Gamora used the Stones to fold reality in half, creating a warp world of merged entities and halving all existence. The warp world incarnation of the Avengers eventually regained the Stones from Gamora and, with the help of Adam Warlock, fixed the damage she had done. Warlock used the Stones to send Gamora to a place where she could heal and redeem herself.

Gamora was not in exile for long. When rumors spread that Thanos had planned his return, his brother Starfox believed that it would be through Gamora, so he created a Dark Guardians squad to track her down. Only it wasn't Gamora that Thanos had planned to use, but Starfox himself. Thanos' lover, Hela, took Starfox to the space observatory called Knowhere to begin the process of transferring Thanos' consciousness into Starfox, only for both teams of Guardians to try to prevent his return. Before the process was over, Gamora killed Starfox, leading to Thanos returning incomplete. During the confrontation, Knowhere, Thanos, and Hela were sucked into a miniature black hole, thereby ending the threat.

"This one may legitimately call herself a mistress of the martial arts."

MANTIS

Mantis: Celestial Madonna

Trained by the Priests of Pama, Mantis is not only an amazing martial artist—she is also mother to the Celestial Messiah!

Mantis gained her martial arts skills from the Priests of Pama, a secret sect of Kree outcasts living on Earth. In the distant past, the priests had opposed their fellow Kree's warlike ways and the attempted genocide of the plant-based life-forms known as the Cotati. The Priests of Pama helped the Cotati survive and in return the Cotati shared the secret of their own telepathic prowess. Mantis' mother was the sister of a Vietnamese crimelord and her father was the German mercenary Gustav Brandt (later known as the villain Libra). When his wife was killed by her brother, Brandt sought sanctuary for himself and his baby daughter with the Priests of Pama. Brandt eventually left his daughter in their care, and she grew up to believe she would be the Celestial Madonna, a powerful being predicted to give birth to the Celestial Messiah. The Priests named her Mantis, due to her exceptional martial arts skills and ability to defeat larger, male opponents. The priests' training gave Mantis amazing control over her body and a knowledge of pressure points—where one touch could incapacitate, or even kill, an opponent.

After her training was finished, the Priests wiped 18-year-old Mantis' mind and cast her out to experience the human world. She eventually met the former Avenger the Swordsman, helping him regain his self-belief and confidence to return to the Avengers' team. Soon after, the Swordsman was killed in battle, but he was reborn as a member of the Cotati, and married Mantis. They left Earth to fulfil their destinies and Mantis bore a child: Sequoia, the Celestial Messiah.

Sequoia remained with the Cotati and Mantis adventured with the likes of the Silver Surfer before an explosion split her into five separate entities: freak, mother, woman, adept, and Avenger. The Mad Titan Thanos killed four, which allowed their memories and powers to be passed on

AVENGERS #114 (AUG. 1973) Mantis' knowledge of martial arts and power points gives her the skill to down opponents far stronger than herself—such as the mighty Thor.

ANNIHILATION CONQUEST: STARLORD #2 (OCT. 2007) Mantis was a founding member of the modern-day incarnation of the Guardians of the Galaxy.

to the sole surviving Mantis. With the Avengers' help, she saved her son from Thanos and defeated the Titan, although he was later revealed to be a clone.

Thanks to her connection to the Cotati, Mantis' skin turned green and her psychic powers increased. When she had a flash of precognition that foresaw evil A.I. Ultron and the hive-minded Phalanx destroying worlds, she returned to the Kree homeworld of Hala. She wanted to be imprisoned at the same time as space traveler Star-Lord and several other would-be heroes so they could come together as an anti-Phalanx taskforce—one that would evolve into the modern-day incarnation of the Guardians of the Galaxy. When the threat was over, Star-Lord asked Mantis to use her mental powers to persuade the team to stay together. Although some left in anger after they discovered Star-Lord and Mantis' ruse, the Guardians endured.

Mantis eventually went her own way. She returned to help the Avengers and Fantastic Four when her son, now calling himself Quoi, assumed his role as Messiah of the Cotati and led them in a fullscale war against the Kree, Skrulls, and humans. Mantis tried to turn her son away from the violent ideals his father had planted inside him but failed. While the Cotati's plans to gain control over all plant life in the universe were stopped, the aftermath left Mantis heartbroken, especially when her son, now a prisoner, claimed he was exactly what she had made him—a messiah.

EMPYRE #4 (AUG. 2020) Mantis returned to help the Avengers when her son assumed his role as the Celestial Messiah. Unfortunately she was unable to stop him from taking a violent path.

Karnak: Magister of Martial Arts

Not only is Karnak trained in a variety of martial arts—he can spot a psychological or physical flaw in any person or object.

Karnak was a member of the Inhuman royal family and the son of Mander, the onetime Magister of the Tower of Wisdom, where the Inhumans' monks and philosophers studied. The Inhumans were the result of the alien Kree genetically manipulating primitive mankind to create a race of beings that would serve them. The Kree eventually abandoned their experiment and the Inhumans chose their own path, living apart from humanity and Kree in the city of Attilan. When Karnak's older brother, Triton, was exposed to the Terrigen Mists—a rite of passage for many Inhumans that gave them amazing abilities—he was transformed into an amphibian requiring water to survive. Mander pleaded for his second son, Karnak, not to undergo the process. Instead, Karnak was sent to the Tower of Wisdom, where he trained to be an expert martial artist and tactician, becoming an advisor to Black Bolt, the Inhumans' ruler.

Karnak's fighting skills allowed him to go head-to-head with heroes such as the Thing, and villains such as Ultron and Mister Sinister. Karnak's deadliest skill is not so much his exceptional fighting prowess, but his ability to find the weak spot in anything: whether it is a supposedly unbreakable wall, or a deadly opponent. He even found a flaw in the afterlife following his own death, allowing him to return.

SECRET WARRIORS #5 (OCT. 2017) Karnak's martial arts skills come from years of physical and spiritual training at the Tower of Wisdom.

"It is my discipline to be able to sense the weakest spot in any object—and my power to shatter it."

KARNAK

DAREDEVIL #5 (DEC. 2016) When Karnak fought Daredevil, he thought the hero's weakness was his blindness—not realizing Daredevil's extra senses had been heightened. That gave Daredevil enough of an edge to defeat the Inhuman.

When the Mad Titan Thanos threatened the Inhumans, Black Bolt destroyed Attilan and released the Terrigen Mists across the Earth, unleashing a hidden generation of new Inhumans —or "Nuhumans" as they became known. Trying to work out the reasons for Black Bolt's act sent Karnak insane, and he committed suicide after telling Queen Medusa he had seen the flaw in all things. He returned through one of the Nuhumans, Lineage, who carried the DNA of all his ancestors inside his body. Karnak had believed himself to be in Hell before using his skills to find a way out—and burst out of Lineage's body. Upon his return, Karnak became advisor to Medusa. When Medusa's new role as Inhuman leader saw her try to bring Nuhuman killer Muse to justice, Karnak came to blows with Daredevil, who was also hunting the villain. While Karnak was defeated, it seemed he had been holding back and could have killed Daredevil with a single touch early in their fight if he had so desired.

When the Inhumans briefly left Earth, Karnak chose to stay and fought alongside the mutant Quake as one of the Secret Warriors, battling Mister Hyde, Taskmaster, and Mister Sinister. During the team's final battle with Sinister, the Tower of Wisdom was destroyed.

When a new Tower of Wisdom was constructed, Karnak followed in his father's footsteps and became its Magister, financing the Tower's existence by working for S.H.I.E.L.D. One mission saw him track down Adam Roderick, a powerful Inhuman boy who had became the focus of a cult and whose powers posed a threat to Earth.

Karnak remains a key member of the Inhumans, teaching a new generation of Nuhumans how to use their abilities.

SECRET WARRIORS #5 (OCT. 2017) Karnak's lightning fast movements and ability to find weak points have enabled him to defeat larger and stronger foes, such as Mister Hyde.

Howard the Duck: Four Feathers of Death!

Howard the Duck accidentally arrived on Earth having left his own world via the Nexus of Infinite Realities—a portal to alternative timelines.

HOWARD THE DUCK #3 (MAY 1976) Howard's new fighting skills allowed him to take on larger foes.

Since arriving on Earth, Howard has been many things: a Private Investigator, a member of the Defenders, and even a presidential candidate. Perhaps his finest hour, however, was when he became a martial arts expert. Howard had been to

HOWARD THE DUCK #3 (MAY 1976) Howard found his martial arts teacher through an advertisement in the *Deadly Feet of Kung Fu* magazine. Master C'haaj also claimed to teach Eastern proverbs for all occasions.

HOWARD THE DUCK #3 (MAY 1976) As a master of quak fu, Howard was more than a match for Count Macho's students.

the movies with his girlfriend, Beverly, and was relaxing in a diner, when an evil kung fu teacher named Count Macho attacked a young child in front of the couple. Howard realized he had to learn how to fight to stand a chance of bringing Count Macho to justice and was fortunate enough to find a teacher—Master C'haaj. It transpired that Count Macho had once been a student of Master C'haaj, but had started to use his teachings to make money. After a brief period of training, Howard became a master of various martial arts thanks to C'haaj's advanced teaching techniques, which taught Howard a lifetime of kung fu, karate, and tai chi skills in just three hours and 17 minutes. Master C'haaj was deeply impressed with Howard and gave him the name of Shang-Op, which (he claimed) translated as the "rising and advancing of a duck." He also believed that Howard's flashing feathered fingers and indomitable courage made him a master of quak fu.

Howard soon learned that Count Macho had kidnapped Beverly. Howard went to face him and, using his newly acquired martial arts prowess, defeated the villainous teacher, who plunged to his death from a skyscraper. Howard's quak fu skills remained with him for some time, helping him defeat the likes of the One-Armed Bandit.

Now operating as a Private Investigator, Howard continues to use his quak fu knowledge to deal with any thugs who cross his path.

"I am the rising and advancing spirit. I… am Shang-Chi, and my journey never ends."

SHANG-CHI

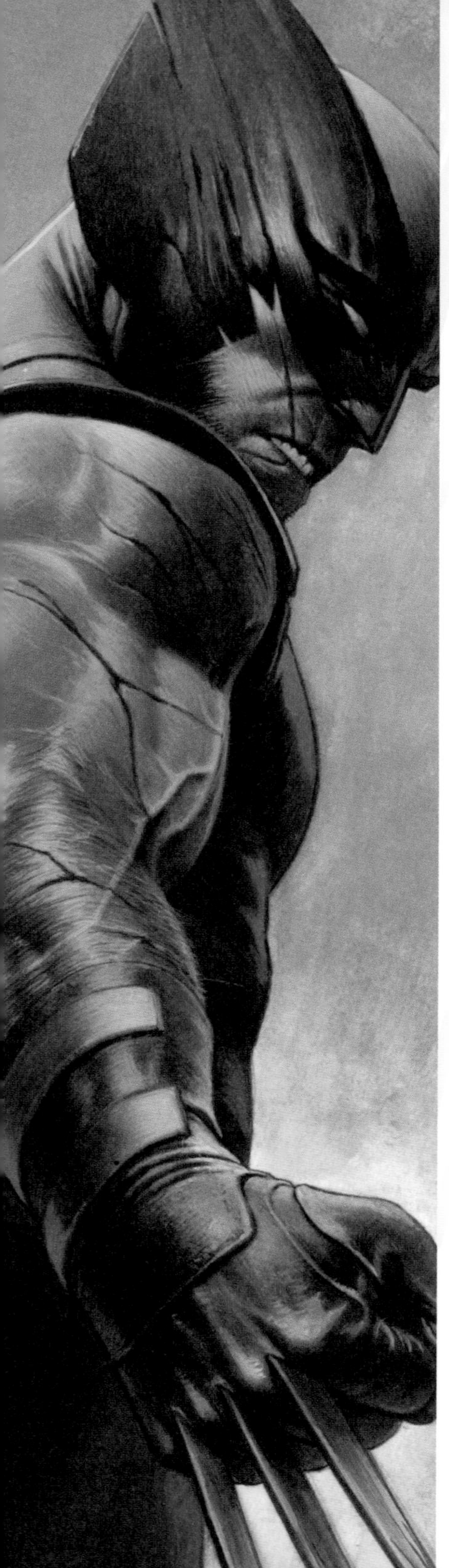

Index

N

O

P

Q

R

S

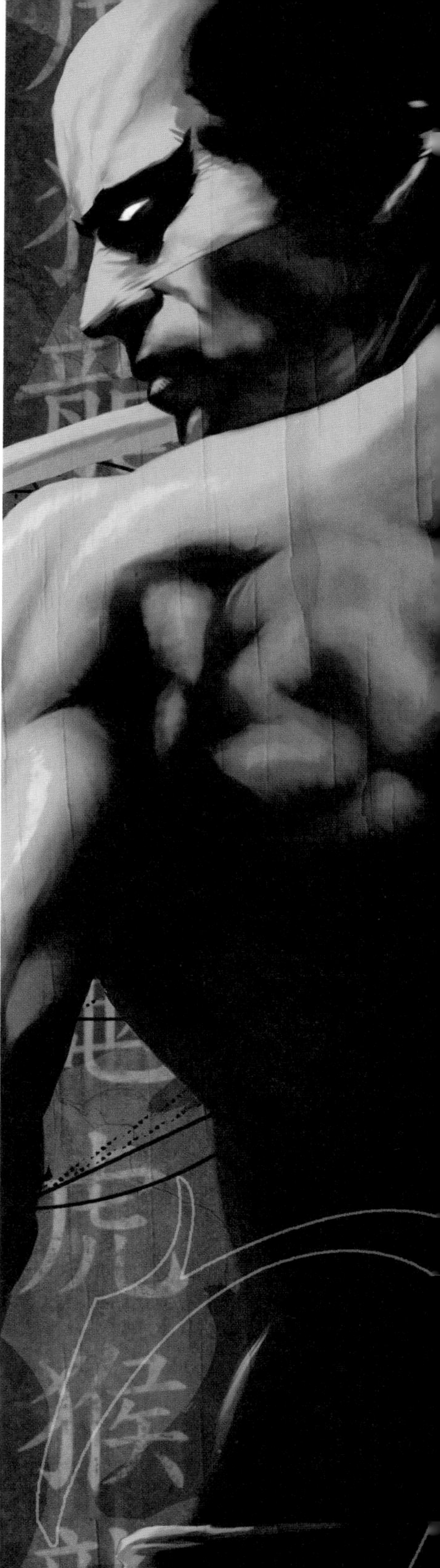

Senior Editor David Fentiman
Senior Designer Anne Sharples
Copy Editor Kathryn Hill
Production Editor Marc Staples
Senior Production Controller Louise Minihane
Managing Editor Sarah Harland
Managing Art Editor Vicky Short
Publishing Director Mark Searle

First American Edition, 2021
Published in the United States by DK Publishing
1450 Broadway, Suite 801, New York, NY 10018

21 22 23 24 25 10 9 8 7 6 5 4 3 2 1
001–321709–May/2021

Published in Great Britain by Dorling Kindersley Limited.
A catalog record for this book is available from the Library of Congress.
ISBN: 978-0-7440-2719-8

DK books are available at special discounts when purchased in bulk for sales promotions, premiums, fund-raising, or educational use.
For details, contact: DK Publishing Special Markets,
1450 Broadway, Suite 801, New York, NY 10018
SpecialSales@dk.com

Printed in China

Acknowledgments
DK would like to thank:
Brian Overton, Caitlin O'Connell, Jeff Youngquist, Joe Hochstein, Darren Shan, and Tom Groneman at Marvel for vital help and advice; Megan Douglass for proofreading; and Vanessa Bird for the index.

The author would like to thank:
Sifu Michael Tse and Sigong Ip Chun

For the curious
www.dk.com

This book is made from Forest Stewardship Council™ certified paper—one small step in DK's commitment to a sustainable future.

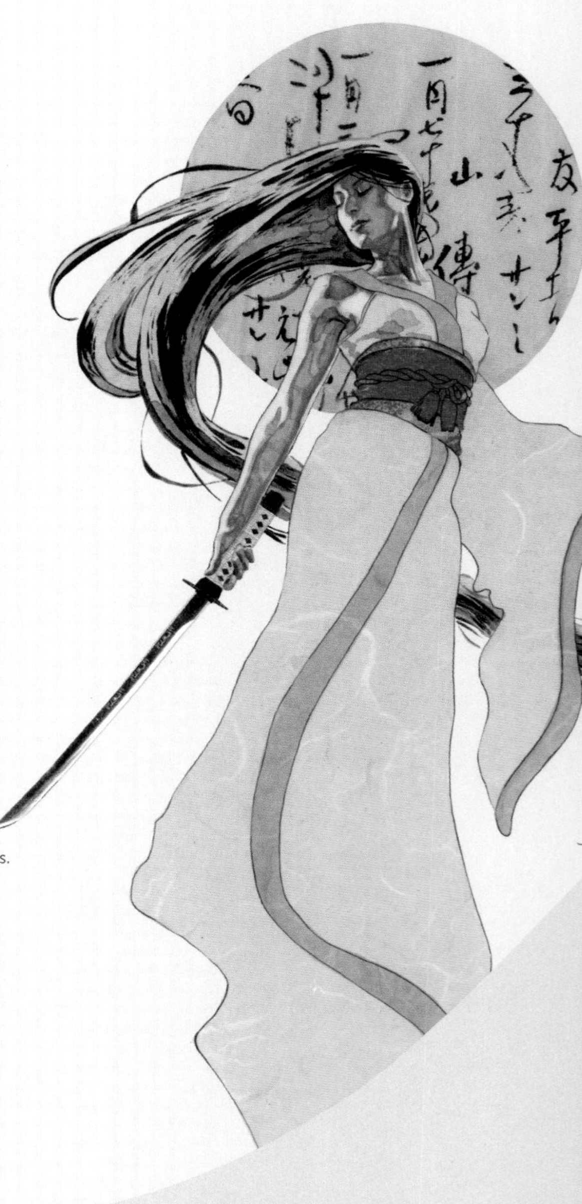